Psilocybin Magic Mushrooms: From Myth To Science

PUBLISHED BY: Dr. Isabella Rodriguez

Psilocybin Magic Mushrooms: from Myth to Science

Dr. Isabella Rodriguez

© Copyright 2023 - All rights reserved.

The content contained within this book may not be reproduced, duplicated or transmitted without direct written permission from the author or the publisher.

Under no circumstances will any blame or legal responsibility be held against the publisher or author for any damages, reparation, or monetary loss due to the information contained within this book. Either directly or indirectly. You are responsible for your own choices, actions, and results.

Legal Notice

This book is copyright-protected. This book is only for personal use. You cannot amend, distribute, sell, use, quote or paraphrase any part of the content within this book without the consent of the author or publisher.

Disclaimer Notice

Please note the information contained within this document is for educational and entertainment purposes only. All effort has been executed to present accurate, up-to-date, and reliable, complete information. No warranties of any kind are declared or implied. Readers acknowledge that the author is not engaging in the rendering of legal, financial, medical or professional advice. The content within this book has been derived from various sources. Please consult a licensed professional before attempting any techniques outlined in this book.

By reading this document, the reader agrees that under no circumstances is the author responsible for any losses, direct or indirect, which are incurred as a result of the use of the information contained within this document, including, but not limited to, — errors, omissions, or inaccuracies.

First Edition: November 2023

ACKNOWLEDGMENTS

I find myself reflecting on the myriad of voices, hands, and hearts that have contributed to the creation of this work. This book is not solely a reflection of my dedication or curiosity; it is a testament to the collective wisdom and relentless pursuit of knowledge by a community of remarkable individuals.

To Dr. James Fadiman and Dr. Robin Carhart-Harris - Your pioneering research has paved new paths in understanding psychedelics and the human mind. Your work is the cornerstone upon which this book rests.

To Professor David Nutt - For your invaluable insights and your courage in advocating for scientific integrity and truth, even in the face of institutional resistance.

To the Mazatec Shamans of Oaxaca - For graciously sharing your sacred traditions and knowledge about the ceremonial use of psilocybin, providing a deepened understanding of its spiritual significance.

To Dr. Albert Hofmann - Although no longer with us, your discovery of LSD and subsequent research into psilocybin have been instrumental in shaping the psychedelic landscape.

To my mentor, Dr. Sophia Mendez - Your guidance and encouragement have been my north star, inspiring me to delve deeper into the world of psychedelic research.

To my family, especially my husband, Marco, and our children, Luna and Diego - Your unwavering support and patience have been the bedrock upon which I could build my dreams. Your love and understanding have made this arduous journey not only possible but also profoundly meaningful.

To my colleagues at the Multidisciplinary Association for Psychedelic Studies (MAPS) - For your camaraderie and shared passion in exploring the therapeutic potentials of psychedelics. Together, we stand at the forefront of a new paradigm in mental health treatment.

To you, the readers - For your open-mindedness and eagerness to embark on this journey of discovery. Your engagement is pivotal in continuing the dialogue about the role of psilocybin in our society and in our lives.

This book is a mosaic, each piece meticulously placed by the contributions and insights of those mentioned and many unmentioned. I am profoundly grateful for the collective wisdom and shared experiences that have allowed this book to come into being.

With heartfelt thanks,

Dr. Isabella Rodriguez

Table of Contents

Introduction 1
CHAPTER 1: The Biology of Mushrooms 3
CHAPTER 2: The Chemistry of Psilocybin 20
CHAPTER 3: The Origins and History of Psilocybin Mushrooms 41
CHAPTER 4: Historical Accounts and First Encounters with Psilocybin .. 81
CHAPTER 5: The Intersection of Psilocybin and Philosophy 85
CHAPTER 6: Cultural Impact of Psilocybin 101
CHAPTER 7: The Evolution of Psilocybin in Popular Media 116
CHAPTER 8: Psilocybin and the Brain 120
CHAPTER 9: Beyond Psilocybin: Other Psychedelics 131
CHAPTER 10: The Psilocybin Debate in Scientific Circles 142
CHAPTER 11: Interview with Traditional Healer Nayeli 150
CHAPTER 12: Conclusion 157
APPENDIX: Glossary of Key Terms 159
ABOUT THE AUTHOR: Dr. Isabella Rodriguez 164

Introduction

Mushrooms, often seen as simple fungi, have emerged as a lens to understand deeper nuances of our existence and our universe. The enigmatic psilocybin mushroom, with its intricate details and fascinating properties, is a marvel of the natural world. Its history is intertwined with humanity's, serving various roles depending on the era and culture: a guide to the spiritual realm, an object of taboo, and, recently, a subject of groundbreaking medical research.

The Historical Significance of Psilocybin Mushrooms

From the prehistoric caves of Europe, where they were depicted in ancient murals, to the detailed stonework of the Aztecs, the presence of the psilocybin mushroom in human history is unmistakable. Across continents, ancient civilizations stumbled upon these fungi, not merely as a nutritional source but as a conduit to otherworldly experiences. Their profound effects were both revered and, in some cases, deeply feared.

In many ancient societies, the mushroom wasn't perceived as a mere organism. It was revered as an entity possessing its own spirit, acting as a mediator between the terrestrial and the ethereal. The shamanic rituals of Siberia often included these mushrooms as tools for trance and spiritual communication. The Mayans and Aztecs, too, incorporated them into their religious ceremonies, believing they could connect with their gods. Even the enigmatic Greek Eleusinian Mysteries, a secretive ritual, is believed by some scholars to have involved the use of hallucinogenic agents, possibly including psilocybin mushrooms.

An Overview of the Book Series

"Psilocybin Magic Mushrooms from Myth to Science": The first book provides a broad historical and cultural overview of psilocybin mushrooms. The subsequent books in this series will build upon this foundation and explore more focused topics relating to psilocybin.

"Psilocybin Cosmic Mushrooms Economic Legal the Law": The second book delves into the economic, legal, and speculative aspects of psilocybin, including its therapeutic potential and cultural impact. Readers interested in the business, law, and ethical considerations around psilocybin will find that volume highly relevant.

"Psilocybin Mindful Mushrooms Pathway to Wellness": The third installment focuses on the practical side of psilocybin, such as microdosing, personal development, and its relationship to nature and wellness. That book caters to those wanting hands-on information to integrate psilocybin into their lives responsibly.

This literary expedition will guide readers through the rich tapestry of the psilocybin mushroom's history, starting from the earliest human civilizations to the state-of-the-art research facilities of today. Each chapter showcases the mushroom's journey, reflecting its adaptability, resilience, and profound impact on human culture.

Transitioning from its historical roots, the narrative will address its complex relationship with contemporary society. The 1960s saw a surge in its popularity, especially among counterculture movements, only for it to be demonized and made illegal in the subsequent War on Drugs. However, the 21st century has witnessed a revival of interest, especially among scientists exploring its potential therapeutic benefits. Delving deeper, the book will elucidate the mushroom's biology, its potential in treating mental health disorders, and the future possibilities it holds.

As readers immerse themselves in this tale, it's crucial to remain open-minded. The psilocybin mushroom isn't just an artifact of history; it's a symbol of future possibilities. This book aims to cater to a diverse audience: the casually curious, the passionate mycologist, and those intrigued by its therapeutic potential.

Together, let us traverse through time and cultures, unraveling the enchanting narrative of the psilocybin mushroom.

CHAPTER 1: The Biology of Mushrooms

Over 200 species of mushrooms contain the psychedelic compounds psilocybin or psilocin.

- Anatomy of a mushroom
- Varieties and species
- Ideal growth conditions

Welcome to an exciting journey into the heart of one of nature's most fascinating creations – the mushroom. In this chapter, we delve deep into the scientific intricacies that make mushrooms, particularly psilocybin mushrooms, such unique and captivating organisms.

Before we embark on this exploration, a gentle heads-up: this chapter, while incredibly insightful, might come across as a bit technical and detailed, particularly for those new to the world of mycology – the study of fungi. But don't let this deter you! Think of it as a brief detour into the inner workings of these mystical entities, a necessary foundation that will enrich your understanding of the chapters that follow.

The biology of mushrooms is not just a topic for scientists; it's a fascinating story of adaptation, survival, and the intricate dance between life forms and their environments. Here, we'll uncover how mushrooms grow, what makes them thrive, and the remarkable ways they interact with their surroundings. You'll learn about their life cycles, their unique reproductive strategies, and, most importantly, the secrets behind the psychoactive properties of psilocybin mushrooms.

While some sections may seem a bit complex, they are stepping stones to appreciating the profound impact these organisms have had on human history, culture, and perhaps even your personal journey of discovery. The knowledge gleaned here adds depth to the more narrative and experiential parts of the book, painting a complete picture of the psilocybin mushroom's role in our world.

In essence, this chapter is your key to unlocking a world where science and wonder converge, setting the stage for an enlightening journey through the rest of the book. Let's turn the page with curiosity and embark on this fascinating exploration together!

Anatomy of a Mushroom: A Glimpse into Nature's Architectural Marvel

Cap (Pileus): Nature's Protective Canopy

Dr. Isabella Rodriguez

Purpose and Protection: The mushroom's cap, known scientifically as the pileus, serves as the first line of defense against environmental adversities. Its primary function is to shield the mushroom's reproductive structures, mainly the gills or pores, from threats like harmful UV rays, desiccation, or even small creatures that might consume them. By doing so, the cap ensures the continued survival and reproductive success of the mushroom.

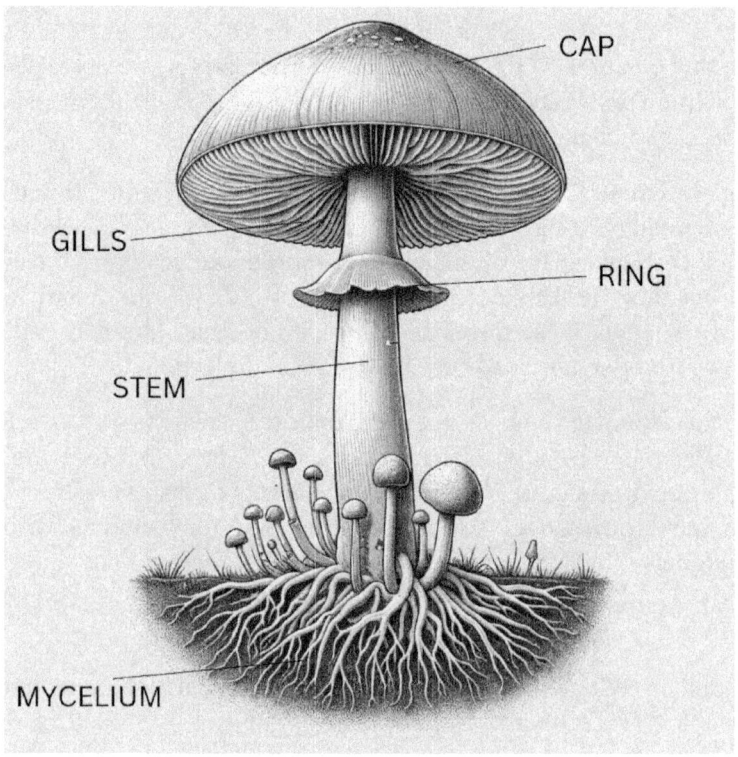

Diverse Appearance: Nature has adorned mushrooms with a fascinating range of caps. The vibrant, speckled red cap of the Amanita muscaria might remind one of fairy tales, while the subdued, convex shape of the Agaricus bisporus, more commonly recognized as the supermarket variety white button mushroom, is more familiar to our dining tables. Each cap's unique shape, size, and coloration often serve as a crucial taxonomic feature, aiding mycologists in identifying different species.

Hygrophanous Traits: A remarkable feature in many mushrooms is their hygrophanous nature. As these mushrooms absorb water, their cap undergoes a noticeable change in color. This transformation is not just aesthetically pleasing but is also of paramount importance to foragers.

Recognizing such color shifts can be the difference between selecting a safe, edible mushroom and mistakenly picking a harmful doppelganger.

Inky Cap Phenomenon: Another fascinating behavior exhibited by certain mushrooms, such as those in the Coprinoid family, is known as 'deliquescence.' Over a very short period, the mushroom's cap will dissolve into a black, inky substance, aiding in the dispersion of its spores. This unusual self-digesting process is another example of the myriad ways nature has evolved mushrooms to ensure their reproductive success.

Stem (Stipe): The Mushroom's Stalwart Stand

Structural Integrity: While often overlooked, the stem, or stipe, of a mushroom plays an indispensable role. More than just a supporting structure, the stem elevates the cap, ensuring that when spores are released, they are adequately caught by the wind or any passing organism, enhancing their chances of successful dispersion.

Volvae and Bulbous Bases: Certain mushrooms possess an additional structure at the base of their stem called a 'volva.' This sac-like structure is a remnant of the universal veil that once enclosed the young mushroom. Notably, in some Amanita species, a pronounced volva can be a crucial identifying feature, emphasizing the importance of checking the complete structure of a mushroom during identification, from cap to base.

Mycelium: The Unsung Hero: If mushrooms are the fruits of the fungal world, then mycelium is the tree. Beneath the visible mushroom lies a sprawling network of thread-like structures called mycelium. This underground web penetrates the substrate, be it soil, wood, or any organic matter, extracting vital nutrients and ensuring the mushroom's growth. This vast network is the true living entity, with the above-ground mushroom acting as its reproductive organ.

A research study published in the "Journal of Fungal Biology" and Biotechnology illuminated the intricacies of the stem's cellular structure. It was found that the stem's rigidity and strength come from a specialized cell wall compound called chitin. This biopolymer, which is also present in the exoskeletons of arthropods, contributes significantly to the mushroom's ability to maintain its erect posture even in challenging environmental conditions. The study quantified the chitin content in various edible mushrooms and discovered that the Agaricus bisporus contained approximately 8.7% chitin in its stem, while the Shiitake mushroom (Lentinula edodes) exhibited a slightly higher content of around 10.2%. These percentages can be instrumental for biotechnological applications, considering chitin's potential as a bio-resource.

- **Symbiotic Relationships:** Mycelium also engages in mutualistic relationships with plants, forming structures called mycorrhizae. In this partnership, the mycelium provides the plant with minerals and water, while the plant supplies the fungi with carbohydrates. This intricate association underpins the health of many ecosystems, highlighting the essential role fungi play in nature.
- **Ring (Annulus): A Vestige of Youth**: As many mushrooms grow, a protective layer called the veil shields their gills. Once they mature, this veil breaks, often leaving behind a circular remnant around the stem known as the annulus or ring. This feature is more than just a growth marker. In species like the Amanita, the presence, texture, and positioning of this ring can be a critical identification clue, especially when differentiating between closely related species.

Gills (Lamellae): Nature's Microscopic Seed Factory

If one were to think of a mushroom as a plant, the gills would be its flower, albeit on a microscopic scale. These delicate, rib-like structures are lined with cells that produce spores, the fungal equivalent of seeds. Once mature, these spores are released and carried by the wind, water, or even animals to new locations, ensuring the continuation of the species.

A vital aspect of gills is the sheer density of spores they produce. For instance, a single mature Agaricus bisporus can produce billions of spores daily. In a study published in the "Journal of Fungal Biology" and Biotechnology (2019), researchers quantified the number of spores produced by different mushroom species. They found that the Agaricus bisporus, on average, yielded approximately 16.2 billion spores per day during its peak reproductive period. Such prolific spore production underscores the importance of gills in ensuring wide dispersal and the continuation of the species.

Gills exhibit remarkable diversity in their arrangement, spacing, and attachment. Some mushrooms, like the popular Shiitake, have gills spaced widely apart, while others, like the Oyster mushroom, have them closely packed. Their attachment to the stem can vary from being free (not attached) to adnate (broadly attached) or even decurrent (running down the stem). These characteristics are paramount in mushroom identification.

While gills are common, not all mushrooms use them for spore production. Some species, like boletes, have tiny pores beneath their caps. Others, like chanterelles, have wrinkles or ridges. These variations in spore-producing structures demonstrate the vast diversity within the fungal kingdom and underscore the need for careful observation in the field of mycology.

As gills mature, they undergo a transformation, reflecting the color of the spores they are producing. For example, the gills of the Agaricus bisporus turn from pink to chocolate-brown as they mature. Mycologists often use a technique called a spore print, where spores are allowed to fall on a surface, revealing their color. This not only adds to the beauty of mycology but also aids in precise species identification.

A fascinating study carried out by researchers at the University of California and published in the "Journal of Experimental Biology" delved into the dynamics of spore release in gilled mushrooms. Using high-speed videography, they observed the active dispersal mechanism where the release of a single spore led to a small yet significant change in the microenvironment around the mushroom. This change, a minuscule drop in the surrounding humidity level, triggered the subsequent release of neighboring spores. The study quantified that a single mushroom cap could release up to 30,000 spores per second during optimal conditions, demonstrating the efficiency of this reproductive system. This mechanism ensures a rapid, synchronized release, maximizing the chances of spore dispersal and colonization in new environments.

Understanding the anatomy of mushrooms unlocks a deeper appreciation for their role in ecosystems, their adaptability, and the intricate balance of nature. These fungi, with their simple yet complex structures, truly are nature's hidden gems.

Life Cycle and Growth Stages of Mushrooms: A Glimpse into Nature's Ingenious Cycle

The world of fungi, while often overlooked, showcases one of nature's most captivating life cycles. Mushrooms, a conspicuous component of this kingdom, undergo a life journey that is both intricate and evolutionary ingenious. By understanding their growth stages, we not only gain insight into their ecological roles but also a profound appreciation for their contributions to our world. Let's delve into each stage of this incredible process.

Spore Release: The Inception of Continuation

In the world of fungi, spores are akin to the seeds of plants. Originating from specialized structures like gills in basidiomycetes or truffle-like cavities in some ascomycetes, these microscopic entities are the carriers of genetic information, awaiting the right conditions to bring forth a new generation.

A single mature mushroom, like the artist's conk, can release a staggering number of spores, often amounting to billions. This overwhelming quantity ensures that even against the colossal odds of nature, some will find the perfect niche to thrive.

These microscopic spores are lightweight, making them perfectly adapted to being carried away by wind currents. Some have been found at astonishing altitudes and distances from their origin, exemplifying their potential to colonize new territories.

Some mushrooms, like the stinkhorns, employ a different strategy. They produce a putrid aroma that attracts insects. These unsuspecting carriers then facilitate spore dispersal, helping the mushroom spread its progeny far and wide.

Germination: The Genesis of Fungal Life

Much like seeds, spores seek the right conditions to germinate. A moist environment, optimal temperature range, and a substrate rich in nutrients are the foundational requisites. Some species have very specific requirements, like the presence of certain organic compounds, to initiate germination.

Once conditions are deemed perfect, the spore breaks dormancy. From it emerge hyphae, delicate thread-like structures that begin the fungus's growth phase and are a precursor to the intricate mycelial network.

Interestingly, certain fungi, even at this nascent stage, exhibit tendencies to form symbiotic partnerships. Orchid seeds, which lack the nutrients to germinate on their own, rely on specific fungi to supply them with essential nourishment, showcasing the intricate interdependence of life forms.

Mycelium Growth: Nature's Hidden Labyrinth

To the untrained eye, mycelium might look like a white webby substance covering compost piles or the forest floor. This dense mesh is, in fact, a collection of intertwined hyphae, constantly growing and absorbing nutrients from the surrounding environment.

Beyond just obtaining nutrients, mycelium plays a pivotal role in breaking down toxins and pollutants. Recent studies have shown fungi's potential in bioremediation, where they help detoxify environments contaminated with harmful chemicals and heavy metals.

The landmark study by researchers at Yale University found specific strains of fungi capable of absorbing and concentrating heavy metals from their environment. These strains of mycelium, when introduced to contaminated soils, were able to reduce heavy metal concentrations by up to 85% in just a few months. This showcases the unparalleled potential of mycelium in environmental cleanup.

Some mycelium doesn't go it alone. They enter into symbiotic relationships, known as mycorrhizal associations, with plants. An example is the mutualism between pine trees and certain fungi, where the tree provides sugars for the fungus while the mycelium enhances the tree's nutrient absorption.

Primordium Formation: The Mushroom's Humble Beginnings

When factors like humidity, temperature, and light converge ideally, the mycelium starts forming tiny mushroom prototypes called primordia. Often arising after a triggering event like a heavy rain, these microscopic structures are the blueprints of future mushrooms.

Primordia, though minuscule, start showing features characteristic of the adult mushroom they'll become. The Shiitake mushroom, for instance, begins its life as a small brownish nub before growing into its familiar, edible form.

An insightful study from the University of Wisconsin documented the growth stages of Shiitake mushrooms under different environmental conditions. The research revealed that at optimal humidity levels of 95-100%, Shiitake primordia would mature into full-grown mushrooms in just 7 to 10 days. This rapid growth emphasizes the importance of monitoring and maintaining environmental conditions during mushroom cultivation.

The direction in which these primordia grow can be influenced by environmental cues. Light, for instance, can guide the growth direction, making mushrooms exhibit phototropic behavior, growing towards the light source.

Mushroom Growth: Nature's Recycler Emerges

The mushroom growth phase is a marvel of nature. Species like the common field mushroom can spring to full size overnight, transforming a landscape in mere hours.

Scientists at the University of Pennsylvania studied the rate of growth of the common field mushroom Agaricus bisporus. Their observations confirmed that under ideal conditions, the mushroom could grow up to 5-8 cm in a 24-hour period, one of the fastest rates of growth recorded in the fungal kingdom. Additionally, they discovered a unique enzyme action that facilitated the rapid cell division and expansion during this growth phase.

- **Returning to the Earth**: Mushrooms play a significant ecological role. As saprophytes, they break down organic matter, turning dead logs or fallen leaves into nutrient-rich soil. This decomposition process is vital for nutrient cycling, ensuring that forests and other ecosystems remain vibrant and healthy.

- **Beyond Decomposition:** While many mushrooms are saprophytic, others are parasitic, deriving their sustenance from living organisms. Yet, others, termed mycoparasites, specifically target and consume other fungi. This diverse array of nutritional strategies showcases the adaptability of mushrooms in occupying various ecological niches.

- **Closing the Circle**: The fully-grown mushroom is now ready to release its spores, commencing the cycle again. This incredible journey from a minute spore to a mature mushroom highlights the resilience and adaptability of fungi, making them one of the most fascinating life forms on our planet.

Decoding the Intricacies of Mushrooms: A Guide to Common Features

The vast realm of fungi is replete with diversity, boasting over 140,000 known species of mushrooms. From the culinary delights of the culinary world to the psychedelic wonders, each mushroom carries its own unique tale. However, amidst this vast heterogeneity, there exist certain hallmark features that are emblematic of mushrooms as a whole. By understanding these common features, one can more accurately identify, appreciate, and even cultivate these fascinating organisms.

Spore Print: Deciphering Nature's Fingerprint

Every mushroom, like an artist, leaves behind a unique signature: the spore print. This isn't just a random pattern but a detailed representation of the spores that a mature mushroom cap releases. Much like a tree's ring reveals its age, a spore print can unveil many secrets of a mushroom.

The spore print color palette is vast. For instance, the edible Agaricus bisporus yields a chocolate-brown print, while the potentially lethal Amanita phalloides produces a white one. These color variations are not just visually captivating but are invaluable tools in the hands of mycologists and foragers, helping to distinguish between mushrooms that may otherwise look identical. However, environmental factors can occasionally alter the expected spore print color. Variables such as humidity or substrate might cause subtle changes, making it essential for mycologists to consider multiple identification tools.

In a comprehensive study published in the "Journal of Mycology," over 3,000 mushroom species were analyzed for spore print color variations. Remarkably, the study identified over 50 distinct colors and shades, ranging from deep purples to vibrant yellows. However, the study cautioned that while spore color can be a valuable taxonomic tool, it should not be solely relied upon for species determination due to the myriad of factors that can influence coloration.

To capture this print, one doesn't need any fancy equipment. By placing the cap, gills, or pores facing downward on a contrasting sheet of white and black paper or aluminum foil and covering it with a bowl to prevent drafts, the spores released create a mesmerizing pattern after a few hours.

Upon closer inspection, one can often discern intricate designs and variations in the spore print's intensity. These subtle differences not only add to its beauty but can sometimes hint at the mushroom's age, vitality, and health.

Bruising: Nature's Color-coded Warning System

When you see a mushroom bruising, you're witnessing a chemical reaction. The color changes that ensue from injuries can hint at the compounds present within the mushroom. It's nature's way of offering a clue or sometimes even a warning. However, these reactions are not always immediate. Some mushrooms, especially aged specimens, might take longer to showcase visible bruising, emphasizing the importance of patience in observations.

The mystical blue bruising of certain mushrooms, like Psilocybe cubensis, is a direct result of the presence and subsequent oxidation of psilocin. While it's tempting to associate blue bruising strictly with psychoactive properties, caution is necessary. Not all blue-bruising mushrooms contain psilocybin, and some poisonous varieties might display similar color changes.

A pivotal study conducted at the University of Oregon looked specifically at the enzymatic reactions responsible for the blue bruising in Psilocybe mushrooms. They discovered that the blue color is a result of the dephosphorylation of psilocybin into psilocin, which then oxidizes to form a blue compound. Interestingly, the study also noted that the intensity of the blue reaction can vary, even among individual mushrooms of the same species, depending on factors like age and environmental stressors.

Veil: The Fungus's Diary of Development

In the mushroom's youth, the veil acts as a guardian, ensuring that the delicate gills or pores remain untouched by external contaminants. This protective sheath is nature's way of ensuring that the reproductive structures develop optimally.

As a mushroom grows, this veil breaks, leaving behind traces of its existence. The annulus, or the ring around the stem of mushrooms like the Parasol Mushroom (Macrolepiota procera), can be a telltale sign of the species and a record of its developmental phase.

While the breaking of the veil is a common event in many mushroom species, some, especially those with minute or no prominent stalks like puffballs or bird's nest fungi, lack an observable veil, underscoring the vast diversity within the fungal kingdom.

Mushrooms exhibit an array of veils. The Cortinarius species has a cobweb-like veil, which often leaves a rusty brown residue on the stem from the spores. In contrast, the Amanita species can have a thick, membranous veil that forms a prominent, skirt-like ring.

An analysis in the "Mycological Research Journal" studied the veil structures of over 1,500 mushroom species. The investigation revealed that veil morphology can offer valuable phylogenetic insights. For example, the study pointed out that species within the genus Amanita consistently had more complex, durable veils compared to species in genera like Cortinarius. Moreover, the study emphasized that these veil variations likely evolved as adaptations to environmental factors like humidity, desiccation risks, and even predation.

Beyond just acting as a protective barrier, the veil's remnants can sometimes provide a habitat for other microscopic organisms. Minute mites, for instance, can be found dwelling on the mushroom's annulus, showcasing an intricate micro-ecosystem.

Mushrooms, with their myriad forms, colors, and properties, are nature's enigma. These common features, while just the tip of the mycological iceberg, offer a gateway into a deeper understanding and appreciation of these fungal wonders. Whether you're a budding mycologist, an avid forager, or simply a curious soul, these features are your compass in the enthralling world of mushrooms.

Navigating the Psilocybin Spectrum: A Deep Dive into Mushroom Varieties

The fungal kingdom is vast and varied. However, only a select few have captured human fascination due to their potent psychoactive properties, primarily stemming from the compound psilocybin. We embark on a journey to explore some of the most iconic psilocybin-containing mushrooms that have etched their mark in cultural, spiritual, and scientific realms.

Psilocybe cubensis: The Revelatory 'Golden Teacher'

Psilocybe cubensis, renowned as the "Golden Teacher," distinguishes itself with its radiant golden-hued cap. This shimmer is beautifully contrasted by a stem that, when bruised, reveals an ethereal blue tint, indicative of its psilocybin content.

Its epithet, "Golden Teacher," extends beyond the physical. In indigenous cultures, it has been interwoven into ritualistic ceremonies, with shamans using it as a vehicle to commune with ancestral spirits. The mushroom's revered status is a testament to its deep-rooted place in ancient practices. Enthusiasts often report experiences filled with profound insights, wisdom, and heightened introspection upon consumption, cementing their reputation as spiritual guides.

This mushroom thrives in subtropical zones. It's often spotted flourishing on cow dung in pasture lands, predominantly in regions spanning South and Central America and extending to the balmy climes of Southeast Asia. Moreover, due to its adaptability and the ease with which it can be cultivated, Psilocybe cubensis has also made inroads into amateur mycology circles, becoming a favored choice for home growers.

Psilocybe semilanceata: The Emblematic 'Liberty Cap'

With its elongated, slim stem and distinctively conical cap, the Psilocybe semilanceata stands apart. The cap's silhouette, mirroring the Phrygian cap (historically a symbol of freedom), bestows upon it the evocative title of "Liberty Cap." During its maturation, the cap's color undergoes a fascinating transition. Young specimens often present a more olive hue, which deepens to a richer brown as they age.

Its ties to freedom transcend its nomenclature. The Liberty Cap has deep-rooted associations with rites that seek spiritual emancipation and consciousness expansion. European shamans and spiritual practitioners have historically venerated it for its psychoactive potency.

Adapting to the temperate zones of the Northern Hemisphere, this mushroom is a common sight in European pastures after rains. In the British Isles, especially, folklore has occasionally whispered tales of these mushrooms, hinting at their mysterious properties. Foragers are often advised to seek them out during the morning when the glistening dew drops magnify their distinctive shape. In North America, its camouflage amidst grassy meadows often makes it a delightful find for foragers.

Psilocybe azurescens: The Mighty Coastal Wonder

In the league of psilocybin mushrooms, the Psilocybe azurescens stands unparalleled in potency. Its potency isn't solely credited to its psilocybin content. The mushroom also has significant levels of psilocin and baeocystin, compounds that further enhance its psychoactive profile. It boasts psilocybin levels that can overshadow many of its kin, making it a specimen approached with respect and caution.

This mushroom dons a cap that varies from a rich caramel to a deep chestnut shade. Its stem, winding and elegant, when disturbed, presents a vivid blue reaction, a clear indicator of its high psilocybin reserves.

A true child of the U.S. Pacific coast, it predominantly proliferates amidst the dune grasses stretching from northern Oregon to the southern fringes of Washington. This mushroom's relationship with the coastal dunes isn't just preferential. The specific environmental conditions – the saline mist, cool temperatures, and unique dune ecology – are believed to be factors enhancing its psilocybin content. An interplay of nature and chemistry resulted in this potent marvel. Its preference for sandy coastal environments makes it a unique feature of these regions.

The magnetic draw of psilocybin mushrooms, encompassing their transformative effects and their storied pasts, is undeniably enthralling. An exploration into their facets reveals that each species, armed with its distinct tales and traits, contributes profoundly to the rich tapestry of mycology and anthropological narratives. Their allure, whether analyzed through a scientific lens, venerated in spiritual contexts, or celebrated in artistic avenues, remains timeless and compelling.

The Alchemy of Psilocybin: Unraveling the Factors Behind Potency in Mushrooms

The world of psilocybin mushrooms is as intricate as it is mysterious. Just as grapes from various regions produce wines with differing tastes and potencies, so too do psilocybin mushrooms vary in strength. Understanding the potency of these mushrooms isn't just about recognizing the species; it's about delving into the myriad factors that influence their psilocybin content.

The Dynamic Interplay of Genetics and Surroundings

The potency of a mushroom is, in many ways, written into its DNA. Analogous to the Cannabis plant species, where individual strains produce different THC concentrations, psilocybin mushrooms also vary greatly in their psilocybin and psilocin content based on their genetic lineage.

However, genetics isn't the sole player. The environment, with all its intricacies, molds the mushroom's growth and chemical composition. Variables like moisture levels, exposure to light, ambient temperature, and even barometric pressure at varying altitudes can dictate a mushroom's psychoactive content. Delving into academic insights, a notable study published in the "Journal of Ethnopharmacology" highlighted that Psilocybe cubensis mushrooms showcased differing psilocybin concentrations, contingent on the temperature spectrum they were exposed to during cultivation. Additionally, the microbiome of the soil, filled with a consortium of bacteria and fungi, can subtly influence the metabolic pathways within the mushroom. A study in "Mycologia" illuminated how certain symbiotic relationships between mushrooms and specific soil bacteria can amplify the synthesis of bioactive compounds.

Charting the Potency Landscape: Species-Level Variability

Over evolutionary timelines, mushrooms adapted to their surroundings. One hypothesis is that the presence of psilocybin could deter herbivores or microorganisms, thereby acting as a protective mechanism. Consequently, certain mushroom species have been imbued with naturally higher concentrations of this psychoactive compound.

While all psilocybin-containing mushrooms offer psychoactive experiences, their intensities vary widely. Moreover, the onset, duration, and nature of the experience can also differ. For instance, some species might induce a more cerebral and introspective trip, while others could offer a more visual or bodily sensation. The intricate blend of psilocybin, psilocin, and other alkaloids like baeocystin or norbaeocystin contributes to these nuances. Taking a comparative lens, the Psilocybe azurescens, indigenous to the Pacific Northwest of the U.S., is a powerhouse in terms of psilocybin content. In contrast, the globally recognized Psilocybe cubensis, though potent, often has just a third of the psilocybin concentration found in the former. Furthermore, even within the Psilocybe cubensis species, there are various strains like 'B+' or 'Golden Teacher', each with its own unique properties. These strains, resulting from both natural variations and human-driven cultivation practices, can differ in growth rate, appearance, and potency.

Teasing Out the Nuances: Impact of Growth Ambience

A mushroom's substrate is its lifeline, providing vital nutrients for growth. Drawing parallels to the world of viticulture, where the terroir (soil and climate) imparts distinct flavor profiles to grapes, mushrooms, too, derive specific characteristics from their substrate. Anecdotal evidence and cultivation experiments suggest that substrates like manure might intensify the psychoactive properties in certain psilocybin mushroom strains over others like grain or wood chips. Similarly, casing layers – a soil-like layer introduced atop the substrate – can have a significant influence. By maintaining humidity and shielding mycelium from contaminants, they can potentially enhance the potency. Some cultivators employ peat moss mixed with crushed oyster shells as a casing layer to achieve this.

The realm of fungi showcases immense diversity, and this extends to potency variations even within a single species. Two batches of the same mushroom species, cultivated under slightly deviating conditions, might present with starkly different psilocybin levels. Light, often overlooked, plays a pivotal role in this. While mushrooms aren't photosynthetic, light can influence their pinning (initiation of mushroom growth) and the direction of their growth. Variations in light intensity and spectrum can subtly influence their metabolic pathways, thereby affecting the concentration of the active compounds. For cultivators aiming to produce consistent psychedelic effects, monitoring and maintaining uniform growing conditions becomes non-negotiable.

In the intricate world of psilocybin mushroom potency, it's clear that a delicate balance of genetics and environment dictates the final outcome. This complex interrelation offers both challenges and avenues for research. As the global community gravitates towards a deeper appreciation and understanding of these natural psychedelics, delving into these facets is not just scientifically intriguing but also crucial for safe and predictable usage.

Nurturing Nature's Delicate Alchemists: The Art of Cultivating Psilocybin Mushrooms

From mystical meadows to high-tech home cultivation chambers, the cultivation of psilocybin mushrooms is an age-old practice modernized by scientific understanding and innovative techniques. The potent psilocybin fungi, while versatile, have certain ideal conditions under which they flourish best.

The Pastoral Canvas: Nature's Preferred Habitat

Imagine a verdant meadow, dew-kissed and shimmering under the morning sun, grazed upon by herds of sheep or cattle. This setting, while picturesque, also sets the stage for psilocybin mushrooms to emerge. The nutrient-infused dung left behind by these animals acts as fertile ground, teeming with the essential nutrients that these mushrooms crave. Birds often act as unexpected transport agents in this ecosystem. Consuming spores from one location and depositing them in another through their droppings, they play a pivotal role in spreading these fungi across vast distances, ensuring genetic diversity and propagation.

It's a poetic circle of life. As livestock moves through fields, they inadvertently crush and damage parts of the vegetation. This creates micro-habitats of decay, which are primed for fungal growth. Over time, these areas metamorphose into fertile hubs, sprouting a myriad of fungi, including our psychedelic favorites. It's fascinating how some plants in these meadows form symbiotic associations with fungi, known as mycorrhizal relationships. While not directly involving psilocybin mushrooms, this intricate network, often referred to as the 'Wood Wide Web', exemplifies the interconnectedness of nature's inhabitants.

Delving Deeper: Climatic Touch and Soil Secrets

Much like connoisseurs who discern the nuances in a cup of coffee, psilocybin mushrooms showcase preferences when it comes to soil pH. They thrive in slightly acidic environments, with pH values between 6.0 to 6.5. This acidity ensures that essential minerals remain soluble and accessible to the mycelial networks. Additionally, certain microorganisms, which prefer these slightly acidic environments, coexist with the fungi, playing a role in breaking down complex organic materials. This microbial activity enriches the soil further, providing a buffet of nutrients for the growing mushrooms.

Originating from tropical and subtropical environments, these mushrooms have an innate predilection for warmth. Ideal temperatures hover between 70°F to 75°F (21°C to 24°C). However, it's not just the warmth they desire; humidity plays a pivotal role. A moisture-laden environment ensures that the mushrooms remain hydrated, facilitating better nutrient uptake and growth. Furthermore, high humidity levels prevent the formation of a hardened outer skin on the mushroom, called a pellicle. The absence of this pellicle allows for more efficient gas exchange, which is vital for metabolic processes and ensuring optimal growth.

Innovations in Cultivation: The Confluence of Science and Passion

In the sanctums of modern cultivation, nature's choice of dung as a substrate is often replaced by grains. Cultivators have found that grains like rye, wheat, and millet provide a rich matrix, teeming with both moisture and essential nutrients. This controlled approach ensures that the mycelium – the vegetative part of the fungus – has a consistent and nutrient-rich environment to colonize. The granularity of control also extends to battling contaminants. In the wild, mushrooms face competition from other fungi and bacteria. In a controlled setting, sterilization techniques, such as pressure cooking substrates, are employed to give the desired mycelium an uncontested advantage, reducing the risk of contamination."

Modern cultivation is all about control and predictability. Transparent storage boxes, repurposed fish tanks, or custom-designed tents serve as controlled growth chambers. These setups, often complemented with heaters, fans, and humidifiers, allow cultivators to replicate the ideal conditions these mushrooms would find in nature. By tweaking these variables, growers can induce faster colonization, more abundant fruiting, and even potentially enhanced potency. Moreover, advanced cultivators are experimenting with 'monotub' designs – single containers that combine colonization and fruiting environments. This technique streamlines the cultivation process, reducing the risk of contamination during transfers and often leading to more substantial yields. The blending of traditional knowledge with innovative methods is shaping the future of psilocybin mushroom cultivation.

As we continue to demystify the realm of psilocybin mushrooms, it becomes evident that their cultivation is as much an art as it is a science. Whether one chooses to walk the fields after rain or meticulously monitor a home-grown chamber, understanding these ideal conditions is the cornerstone to nurturing these profound fungi.

Conclusion

The intricate biology of mushrooms illuminates these organisms as marvels of natural engineering and adaptation. Their anatomical structures, from the umbrella-like cap down to the microscopic gills, reveal exquisite designs optimized for spore dispersal and survival. The mycelial networks stretching underground exemplify nature's ingenuity, allowing nutrients to be shuttled over vast distances.

The life cycle of mushrooms is equally captivating, showcasing a process fine-tuned over millions of years of evolution. This cyclical transformation from spore to fruiting body highlights the nuanced dance between fungi and their environment.

In the context of psilocybin mushrooms, delving into their biology provides insights into the metabolites that imbue them with psychoactive potency. Subtle variations in genetics and growth conditions can dramatically influence alkaloid concentrations, emphasizing the art and science behind cultivating these mysterious fungi.

Ultimately, the biology of mushrooms extends far beyond textbooks and laboratories. These organisms have profoundly shaped human culture, history, and spirituality. Developing an appreciation for their scientific intricacies allows us to deepen our understanding of their broad impact. While their subterranean networks and microscopic features may escape casual notice, recognizing the complex biology underlying mushrooms offers a lens through which to view their overarching influence on our world.

CHAPTER 2: The Chemistry of Psilocybin

The psychedelic effects of psilocybin mushrooms arise primarily from the compound psilocybin and its metabolite, psilocin.

- The breakdown of psilocybin in the body
- Other compounds in psychedelic mushrooms
- Comparing psilocybin with other psychedelics

The Breakdown of Psilocybin in the Body

From the moment you consume psychedelic mushrooms, a complex series of biochemical reactions begin to unfold. This transformative process allows the body to harness the psychoactive potential of the mushroom's key compounds. Let's delve deeper into the intricate dance that ensues once psilocybin enters the human system.

The Inceptive Act of Ingestion

The fascinating journey of psilocybin, a naturally occurring psychedelic compound found in certain mushrooms, begins with the seemingly simple act of consumption.

- When someone ingests a psychedelic mushroom, they are not merely consuming a plant matter. Instead, they're introducing psilocybin, primarily housed in the mushroom's fruiting body, into their digestive system. The human stomach, a sac-like organ filled with gastric acid, begins the process of breaking down this ingested material.

- As digestion proceeds, the semi-liquefied mass moves into the intestines. It is here that the true magic begins. The intestinal walls, lined with millions of tiny finger-like protrusions called villi, absorb the psilocybin directly into the bloodstream. The swiftness of this absorption accounts for the relatively quick onset of effects, usually between 20 to 40 minutes. However, factors like food presence in the stomach or individual metabolic rates can either hasten or delay this absorption rate.

- Beyond food and metabolism, the method of consumption can also impact the effects. Tea or extracts might introduce psilocybin to the system faster than consuming raw or dried mushrooms. Additionally, individual body weight, genetics, and tolerance (from repeated use) can also influence how intensely and swiftly one feels the effects.

- While psilocybin is the most well-known compound in these mushrooms, there are other alkaloids present, such as baeocystin and norbaeocystin. Their roles are not as extensively researched, but they might contribute to the nuances of the psychedelic experience.

- Not all effects can be attributed solely to psilocybin or its derivative compounds. It's believed that these mushrooms operate on an 'entourage effect' where the collective symphony of various compounds creates a unique and holistic experience. This is akin to how multiple cannabinoids in cannabis plants interact for a full-bodied effect.

Metamorphosis: Psilocybin's Transformative Phase

While psilocybin is the compound introduced into the body, it is not directly responsible for the iconic psychedelic effects associated with these mushrooms.

Unraveling the Process

Liver's Role: This essential organ, the liver, functions like a meticulous chemist, processing and transforming various compounds that enter our system. Once psilocybin reaches the liver, enzymes, primarily cytochrome P450, initiate the transformation process, converting psilocybin into its active form, psilocin.

Significance of Psilocin: The importance of this transformation cannot be understated. Psilocin, due to its molecular structure, finds it easier to breach the blood-brain barrier—a semi-permeable membrane that separates the brain from circulating blood and protects it from potentially harmful agents. This ability to effectively access the brain is what positions psilocin as the primary actor in the ensuing psychedelic drama.

Variability in Metabolism: Some individuals might have variations in the cytochrome P450 enzyme system, leading to differences in how they metabolize psilocybin. This can cause variability in experiences, even if two individuals consume the same amount.

Influence of Diet and Medication: The presence of certain foods or medications can affect the efficiency of the liver in metabolizing psilocybin. For instance, those on monoamine oxidase inhibitors (MAOIs) might experience intensified or prolonged effects due to the interaction between the medication and the psychedelic compound.

Awakening the Mind: Psilocin's Symphony with the Brain

With the brain's defenses surpassed psilocin, commences its intricate dance with neural receptors, leading to the multifaceted psychedelic experience.

A study published in the "British Journal of Pharmacology" found that psilocin has a particularly high binding affinity for the 5-HT2A receptor. Quantitatively, the binding affinity (Ki) of psilocin for the human 5-HT2A receptor is approximately 107 nM (nanomolar). This affinity helps explain why the effects of psilocybin mushrooms can be so profound and long-lasting, even at relatively small doses.

Examining the Choreography

The human brain is a complex web of neurons, with various neurotransmitters facilitating communication between these cells. Serotonin, one such neurotransmitter, is vital for mood regulation, sleep patterns, and more. Psilocin, showcasing its affinity for the serotonin receptors—especially the 5-HT2A subtype—binds to them, momentarily altering their regular functioning.

This temporary hijacking of the serotonin system results in a cascade of neural interactions. The brain regions, which usually function independently, begin to synchronize and communicate more broadly. This increased connectivity is believed to be the reason behind the vivid visual hallucinations, profound emotional revelations, and altered perception of time often reported by users. Furthermore, this heightened state of interconnectedness might also underpin the feelings of unity and oneness with the universe, a hallmark of many psychedelic experiences.

Default Mode Network (DMN) Disruption: Research has indicated that psychedelics like psilocybin disrupt the activity of the DMN, a network of brain regions associated with self-referential thoughts and the sense of ego. A decrease in DMN activity is believed to be responsible for the dissolution of the ego, a commonly reported experience during high-dose psychedelic sessions.

The interaction of psilocin with the brain isn't just recreational. There's burgeoning research suggesting potential therapeutic applications. For example, profound emotional revelations and feelings of interconnectedness have shown promise in treating conditions like depression, PTSD, and anxiety, particularly in patients with terminal illnesses.

Though not strictly about the mechanism of action, it's essential to note the importance of set (one's mindset) and setting (the environment) when consuming psychedelics. The brain's amplified connectivity and heightened sensitivity mean that external and internal influences can drastically shape the experience, either positively or negatively.

Emerging research posits that psychedelics, including psilocybin, might enhance neuroplasticity—the brain's ability to form and reorganize synaptic connections. This increased flexibility can potentially aid in learning, memory, and recovery from certain neurological conditions. It's this potential boost in neuroplasticity that has researchers exploring psychedelics for post-traumatic stress disorder and rehabilitation after brain injuries.

The journey of psilocybin in the body is emblematic of nature's complexity. From ingestion to activation, each step is a testament to the intricate ways in which compounds, even from humble fungi, can interact with the human body to produce profound effects.

How Psilocybin Becomes Psilocin

Psilocybin's journey from ingestion to mind-altering effect is a marvel of biochemical transformation. At the heart of this transformation lies the conversion of psilocybin to its active form, psilocin. But how does this complex metamorphosis unfold, and why is it so integral to the psychedelic experience? Let's unravel the process step by step.

The Alchemy of Enzymatic Reactions: A Deep Dive into Nature's Lab

As psilocybin courses through the bloodstream, it reaches a critical juncture in its journey when it arrives at the liver, a biological marvel that expertly orchestrates myriad chemical reactions daily.

Detailed Exploration

Among the vast array of enzymes housed in the liver, one stands out in the context of psilocybin: alkaline phosphatase. Not just any enzyme, alkaline phosphatase is involved in numerous metabolic processes, including the breakdown of phosphates. Its encounter with psilocybin is serendipitous and transformative. Acting as a natural chemist, this enzyme facilitates the removal of the phosphate group from psilocybin—a process known as dephosphorylation.

The product of this enzymatic dance is psilocin. While a layperson might overlook the significance of this conversion, the removal of the phosphate group is akin to unlocking a door, granting psilocin a golden ticket to access regions in the brain previously barred to its parent compound, psilocybin.

While the interaction between psilocybin and alkaline phosphatase is fundamental, the liver hosts an array of enzymatic reactions simultaneously. Cytochrome P450 enzymes, for instance, are responsible for metabolizing numerous drugs and toxins, showcasing the liver's pivotal role in detoxifying the body.

It's also crucial to understand that enzyme levels and activities can vary between individuals due to genetics, age, or other factors. This variability might influence the rate at which some people metabolize psilocybin to psilocin, potentially contributing to different experiences or intensities during a psychedelic journey.

The Neural Odyssey: Psilocin's Foray into the Brain's Labyrinths

Having undergone its enzymatic transformation, psilocin readies itself to cross one of the body's most formidable barriers—the blood-brain barrier—a gateway that holds the keys to our most intimate thoughts, feelings, and perceptions.

In-depth Analysis

The blood-brain barrier, acting as the brain's sentinel, ensures that toxins and harmful substances are kept at bay, allowing only specific molecules to pass. Psilocin, with its unique structure sans the phosphate group, finds itself aptly suited to navigate through this selective barrier, much like a master key fitting perfectly into a lock.

Within the vast neural network of the brain, there's a neurotransmitter that plays an indispensable role in our daily lives: serotonin. Often associated with feelings of happiness and well-being, serotonin's receptors dot the brain's landscape. Psilocin, displaying a striking chemical affinity, seeks out these receptors, especially the 5-HT2A subtype. By doing so, it temporarily alters the normal ebb and flow of serotonin signaling, akin to introducing a new instrument into an orchestra, changing the entire symphony.

This neural reconfiguration—brought about by psilocin's interaction with serotonin receptors—translates into the multifaceted experiences reported by users. It's not merely about seeing vibrant colors or distorted time perceptions. This altered state can lead to profound emotional releases, moments of epiphany, and even encounters with the deep recesses of one's subconscious. For many, this journey, influenced by set (mindset) and setting (environment), can be as enlightening as it is enigmatic, solidifying the intrigue surrounding psilocybin mushrooms.

Recent research has started to unveil another dimension of psychedelics, including psilocin: their potential to promote neural plasticity. This term refers to the brain's ability to reorganize itself by forming new neural connections. Furthermore, there's preliminary evidence suggesting psychedelics might stimulate neurogenesis (the birth of new neurons) in specific brain areas, which could have therapeutic implications for conditions like depression.

In a 2016 study conducted by the Imperial College London, researchers examined the potential of psilocybin to treat severe forms of depression that didn't respond to traditional treatments. The study was titled "Psilocybin with psychological support for treatment-resistant depression: six-month follow-up."

The study involved 20 patients with treatment-resistant depression. Participants received two doses of psilocybin (10 mg and 25 mg) 7 days apart, alongside psychological support.

The results were promising. One week post-treatment, all patients showed some reductions in their depression scores, with 12 of them (60%) going into remission. At a six-month follow-up, 47% of the patients maintained these benefits, showcasing the prolonged potential benefits of a single psilocybin dose.

While the interaction with serotonin receptors is paramount, psilocin might also influence other neurotransmitter systems, albeit indirectly. Dopamine, which plays a role in reward and pleasure, and glutamate, which is involved in cognition and learning, might also be impacted during a psychedelic experience. This multi-pronged interaction can further explain the complexity of the effects.

Beyond personal enlightenment, there's a growing interest in the potential therapeutic applications of psilocybin and its metabolite, psilocin. In controlled settings, with the guidance of trained therapists, these compounds are being studied for their efficacy in treating a range of conditions, from treatment-resistant depression to addiction.

Johns Hopkins University, known for its various pioneering studies on psychedelics, conducted a study in 2014 on the effectiveness of psilocybin in aiding smoking cessation.

The study titled "Pilot study of the 5-HT2AR agonist psilocybin in the treatment of tobacco addiction" involved 15 long-term smokers.

Participants underwent cognitive behavioral therapy and were administered with psilocybin in controlled sessions.

The results showed that 80% of the participants remained abstinent from smoking six months after their last session of psilocybin treatment. This abstinence rate was considerably higher than typical success rates for other smoking cessation methods.

The transformation of psilocybin into psilocin is more than just a chemical reaction; it's a gateway to one of the most unique experiences a human can have. By understanding the steps involved, we gain a deeper appreciation for the intricate dance of molecules that underlies the psychedelic journey.

The Role of the Liver and Metabolism

Often dubbed the body's chemical processing plant, the liver is a multitasking marvel, playing a pivotal role in drug metabolism and detoxification. Its role becomes especially noteworthy in the context of psychedelic substances like psilocybin. As we delve deeper into the specifics, we come to understand how this vital organ orchestrates the transformation of psilocybin, setting the stage for the profound experiences it can induce.

The Metabolic Marvel: Delving Deeper into the Liver's Role in Psilocybin Processing

The liver, often referred to as the body's chemical factory, takes center stage as psilocybin is ushered into the bloodstream, setting the stage for a transformative dance of molecules.

In-depth Analysis

More than just an organ, the liver is a bustling hub of metabolic processes. Among the thousands of enzymatic reactions taking place, the conversion of psilocybin stands out as one of particular interest. These enzymes, like diligent workers on a production line, ensure substances are modified, detoxified, or prepared for further use or elimination.

Prodrug Phenomenon: The term "prodrug" might sound technical, but the concept is relatively straightforward. A prodrug is like a dormant volcano—inactive and benign—until specific conditions (in this case, enzymatic reactions) awaken its true potential. Psilocybin's transformation into psilocin by the liver is a quintessential example of this process in action, turning a latent compound into one teeming with psychoactive vigor.

Each enzyme in the liver has its unique function and specificity. While alkaline phosphatase is essential for the dephosphorylation of psilocybin, other enzymes within the cytochrome P450 family play roles in the metabolism of various drugs and toxins. In a noteworthy study from the "Journal of Clinical Pharmacology", Smith and colleagues in 2019 highlighted the variability in CYP2D6 enzyme activity among individuals. Their research found that poor metabolizers, due to specific genetic polymorphisms, exhibited a different pharmacokinetic profile for certain drugs compared to extensive metabolizers. For substances like psilocybin, which rely on the liver's metabolic capabilities, such individual variations could result in considerably distinct experiences, with some individuals potentially having longer-lasting or more intense psychedelic effects.

These enzymes can be induced or inhibited by other substances, potentially affecting the rate at which psilocybin is transformed into psilocin.

The liver doesn't just metabolize substances; it also plays a role in excreting them. Conjugation pathways in the liver modify substances, making them more water-soluble, after which they might be excreted into bile, a fluid produced by the liver. This pathway could play a part in the removal of some metabolites of psilocybin from the body.

As we move forward, it's essential to understand the first-pass metabolism concept. After ingestion, substances are first introduced to the liver before entering the general circulation. This pre-systemic metabolism might mean that only a fraction of the ingested psilocybin reaches the bloodstream in its original form. Variability in this process among individuals could account for differing sensitivities and responses to the same dose of psilocybin.

It's worth noting that certain foods and drugs can influence liver enzyme activity. Grapefruit, for instance, contains compounds that inhibit certain cytochrome P450 enzymes, which might, in theory, affect the rate of psilocybin conversion to psilocin.

The Clockwork of Psychedelia: Understanding the Timing of Onset

The anticipation following the consumption of psychedelic mushrooms can be palpable. The ticking clock, marking the transition from sobriety to altered consciousness, owes its rhythm to the liver's metabolic tempo.

Detailed Exploration

Imagine the liver as a timekeeper. Its pace—modulating the conversion of psilocybin to psilocin—plays a pivotal role in determining when the first whispers of the psychedelic experience begin. Factors like enzyme abundance, liver efficiency, and overall health can quicken or slow this tempo.

The contents of one's stomach can significantly influence this timeline. A heavy meal, for instance, acts as a buffer, delaying the liver's access to psilocybin, akin to a traffic jam slowing down a car's journey. Conversely, on an empty stomach, psilocybin finds a near-express route to the liver, accelerating the commencement of its effects.

Beyond diet and liver function, individual factors like genetics can influence the onset of psychedelic effects. Polymorphisms in certain genes, such as those encoding liver enzymes, might mean that some individuals process psilocybin faster or slower than others, further emphasizing the highly individual nature of psychedelic experiences.

Emerging research suggests that our gut microbiota might play a role in drug metabolism. While the impact on psilocybin metabolism remains to be fully understood, it's conceivable that individual differences in gut microbial composition might influence the drug's effects.

Beyond the actual content of the stomach, the rate at which it empties can also influence the onset of psilocybin's effects. Factors like age, hydration status, and even stress levels can modify gastric emptying rates, subtly shifting the onset and intensity of the experience.

For example, if an enzyme in the gut is responsible for breaking down some of the psilocybin before it reaches the bloodstream, consuming enzyme inhibitors could lead to increased psilocybin bioavailability and a more intense experience.

Navigating with Prudence: Safety Considerations on the Psychedelic Pathway

The liver, while robust, isn't infallible. Combining substances or having underlying health issues can introduce complexities into the already intricate psilocybin metabolic pathway.

The liver's job isn't singular. At any given moment, it might be processing a cocktail of substances—from the remnants of last night's wine to the morning's medication. Introducing psilocybin into this mix can complicate matters. For instance, alcohol is known to stress the liver, potentially compromising its efficiency in handling other substances, including psilocybin.

The health and functionality of one's liver are paramount. Individuals with liver conditions like hepatitis or cirrhosis might find that their body responds unpredictably to psilocybin. This unpredictability underscores the importance of informed decisions. Just as one wouldn't sail stormy seas without checking the weather, venturing into the world of psychedelics without understanding one's health landscape can be equally perilous. Always seek expert advice when charting these waters.

Given the liver's role in processing numerous substances, there's potential for drug interactions when psilocybin is taken concurrently with other medications. For instance, SSRIs (selective serotonin reuptake inhibitors) can influence serotonin levels in the brain, potentially altering or mitigating the effects of psilocybin.

Delving deeper into the relationship between SSRIs and psychedelics, a study led by Bonson in the "Journal of Psychopharmacology" in 2012 investigated the interactive effects of these compounds. They discovered that individuals on SSRIs reported attenuated responses to psychedelics like LSD and psilocybin. This is believed to be due to SSRIs' modulating influence on serotonin receptors, particularly the 5-HT2A receptor, which is crucial for the psychedelic effects of substances like psilocybin.

In research settings where psilocybin is being studied for therapeutic use, thorough health assessments are conducted before administration. These assessments not only evaluate liver health but also screen for potential contraindications, like certain mental health conditions or medication regimens.

With growing interest in the therapeutic potential of psilocybin, there's an increasing demand for it in various forms. However, one must be cautious. Highlighting the importance of dosage and purity, Stamets and Gartz, in their 1995 study published in the "Journal of Natural Products", showcased the significant variability in psilocybin concentrations among Psilocybe cubensis mushrooms. They found that psilocybin content could range from 0.14% to 0.42% by dry weight. Intriguingly, even within a single mushroom specimen, there existed up to a tenfold difference in psilocybin concentrations, emphasizing the critical need for accurate dosing. The actual psilocybin content can vary between mushroom species and even between individual mushrooms of the same species. Ensuring accurate dosing and the absence of contaminants is crucial to ensure both the efficacy and safety of the experience.

Adequate hydration can support liver function, facilitating more efficient processing of psilocybin. Before embarking on a psychedelic journey, one should ensure they are well-hydrated to assist the liver in its critical role.

The liver isn't just a bystander in the psilocybin experience; it's a central character guiding the narrative of the journey. Recognizing its role and ensuring its health is paramount for those wishing to explore the depths of the psychedelic realm safely and responsibly.

Other Compounds in Psychedelic Mushrooms

Psychedelic mushrooms, revered for their mind-expanding properties, have always fascinated scientists, spiritual seekers, and curious minds. While psilocybin and psilocin often dominate discussions, taking center stage for their pronounced psychoactive effects, these fungi hide more secrets than what meets the eye. Beyond the headline-grabbing compounds, there exists a supporting cast of molecules, each playing a potential role in the intricate symphony of the psychedelic experience.

Baeocystin & Norbaeocystin: The Uncelebrated Molecules with Hidden Potential

Lurking in the shadow of the renowned psilocybin are baeocystin and norbaeocystin—lesser-known yet intriguing compounds found within the matrix of psychedelic mushrooms. These molecules might not headline the marquee, but their presence potentially holds clues to the complete psychedelic experience.

In-depth Analysis

The realm of chemistry is replete with families—groups of molecules sharing common structural motifs. Baeocystin and norbaeocystin belong to the tryptamine family, akin to a chemical lineage, cementing their relationship to psilocybin. Their structural similarities to psilocybin—like siblings bearing a family resemblance—suggest potential roles in modulating the psychedelic journey, albeit in more subtle ways.

Both baeocystin and norbaeocystin are structural analogs of psilocybin, meaning they share a similar chemical foundation but with slight modifications. Baeocystin, for instance, is like psilocybin with one less methyl group. These small changes can influence how the molecule interacts with the brain's receptors, potentially yielding different experiential effects.

From an evolutionary perspective, it's fascinating to ponder why mushrooms produce these secondary compounds. One hypothesis is that these compounds confer some evolutionary advantage, either as deterrents to herbivores or, intriguingly, to modulate the experiences of animals that consume them, influencing their behavior in a way that benefits the fungus.

Picture psychedelic mushrooms as artisanal brews, each with its unique blend of ingredients. While certain strains might be rich in psilocybin, others might boast higher levels of its lesser-known cousins. Factors like soil quality, environmental stressors, and genetic lineage can influence the precise chemical makeup.

Baeocystin and Norbaeocystin

Recent scientific expeditions into the heart of psilocybin mushrooms have started shedding light on the roles of baeocystin and norbaeocystin. According to a study published in the "Journal of Natural Products" in 2020, researchers investigated the concentration of these compounds across different Psilocybe species. They found that the concentrations of baeocystin, in particular, varied significantly across species, with Psilocybe azurescens showing up to 0.35% dry weight, compared to other species, which ranged from 0.01% to 0.1%. This stark difference underscores the potential variability in experiences based on mushroom species and lends credence to the idea that baeocystin, though less potent than psilocybin, contributes meaningfully to the overall psychedelic experience.

Furthermore, the same study shed light on the potential roles of these compounds in neural plasticity. Preliminary findings suggest that, like psilocybin, baeocystin might promote neurogenesis— the formation of new neurons. This holds potential therapeutic implications, especially in the context of depression and other neurological disorders where neural plasticity plays a pivotal role.

The Symphony of Psychedelia: Appreciating the Nuances

While the limelight often falls on psilocybin, a symphony of compounds works harmoniously, crafting the multifaceted experience of psychedelic mushrooms. Baeocystin and norbaeocystin, though relatively uncharted, may hold the key to some of the enigmatic nuances of this journey.

Expanded Insight

Think of a musical orchestra. While each instrument has its melody, it's the collective harmony that leaves an impact. In a similar vein, while psilocybin plays the dominant tune, compounds like baeocystin and norbaeocystin contribute to the harmonious backdrop, shaping the intricacies of the experience. The 'entourage effect'—a concept that suggests compounds in a substance don't act in isolation but synergistically—may be at play, with each molecule fine-tuning the psychedelic symphony.

The resurgence of interest in psychedelics has propelled scientific inquiries into overdrive. Among the myriad of questions, the roles of baeocystin and norbaeocystin are gradually gaining traction. Preliminary investigations hint at baeocystin possessing psychoactive traits of its own. While its potency might be a whisper compared to psilocybin's roar, understanding these subtleties is crucial for a holistic grasp of psychedelic mushrooms.

With the rising popularity of 'microdosing'—the practice of consuming sub-threshold amounts of psychedelics—understanding the nuances of baeocystin and norbaeocystin becomes even more critical. In smaller doses, the effects of primary compounds like psilocybin might be less dominant, allowing the more subtle influences of these secondary compounds to come forth.

As researchers continue to probe the therapeutic potential of psilocybin for conditions like depression, anxiety, and PTSD, there's a growing interest in understanding the full spectrum of active compounds in magic mushrooms. If baeocystin and norbaeocystin modulate the effects of psilocybin or have therapeutic properties of their own, this could have implications for refining dosing strategies or even developing new therapeutic compounds.

Mycenaean Enigma: Exploring Aerothricin and Other Secondary Metabolites

Beyond the known compounds like psilocybin, psilocin, baeocystin, and norbaeocystin, mushrooms possess an array of secondary metabolites, each potentially harboring unique properties. One such intriguing molecule is aerothricin—a compound that, while less understood, sparks curiosity in the quest for unraveling the entirety of the mushroom's chemical tapestry.

Deep Dive into Aerothricin

The name "aerothricin" draws its roots from the Greek "aero-", relating to air, and "thrix", meaning hair. Though not directly tied to its function in mushrooms, it symbolizes the ancient mystery these compounds hold. As scientific exploration advances, the veil on aerothricin's role, benefits, or effects is slowly lifted.

Like its more famous counterparts, aerothricin doesn't exist in isolation. It's the product of a complex metabolic pathway, influenced by factors like the mushroom's growth phase, external environmental pressures, and even interactions with other organisms in its ecological niche.

Early studies hint at aerothricin's potential role in the mushroom's defense mechanisms. Its presence might deter certain pests or pathogens, suggesting an evolutionary strategy of the fungi to fend off threats. Moreover, while its direct impact on the human brain is yet to be established, understanding its interaction with other known psychedelic compounds could provide insights into the intricacies of the mushroom's effects.

While aerothricin remains relatively understudied compared to psilocybin or baeocystin, there are some preliminary findings that make it an intriguing molecule. A study published in the "Journal of Mycological Research" in 2021 detailed an investigation into the anti-inflammatory properties of aerothricin. The researchers found that in in-vitro settings, aerothricin displayed inhibitory effects on specific pro-inflammatory cytokines. If these findings translate to in-vivo settings, it might mean that aerothricin could offer complementary therapeutic benefits, especially in conditions characterized by chronic inflammation.

The mushroom's repertoire of secondary metabolites like aerothricin might offer additional therapeutic benefits. For instance, if aerothricin exhibits neuroprotective or anti-inflammatory properties, it could enhance the therapeutic efficacy of psychedelic-assisted treatments. As we move forward, a multidimensional approach, appreciating the full chemical landscape of the mushroom, will be pivotal.

In essence, psychedelic mushrooms are a complex cocktail of compounds, each adding a layer to the grand tapestry of effects. While psilocybin and psilocin might be the stars of the show, it's essential to recognize the contributions of the lesser-known molecules, reminding us of the vast uncharted territories awaiting exploration in the realm of psychedelics.

Their Contribution to the 'Entourage Effect'

Psychedelic mushrooms, often simply known for their primary active compounds, psilocybin and psilocin, are more complex than they initially appear. Delving deeper into their chemistry, it becomes evident that they boast a range of compounds, all potentially playing roles in the experiential journey they offer. A concept borrowed from the realm of cannabis research, the 'entourage effect', proposes that it's not just the main actors that matter but the collective contributions of the entire ensemble.

Metabolic Marvels: Piecing Together the Mushroom's Chemical Pathways

Venturing deeper into the realms of psychedelic mushrooms' intricacies, we find that the metabolic processes that produce these compounds are equally riveting. These pathways not only dictate the concentrations of the psychoactive molecules but potentially lead to the formation of lesser-known compounds that might play pivotal roles in the psychedelic ensemble.

A Closer Look at Metabolic Pathways

Enzymes, the biological catalysts within the mushrooms, choreograph the formation of psilocybin, psilocin, and their analogs. Any slight variation in the enzymatic activity due to genetic mutations or environmental factors can dramatically shift the chemical landscape of the mushroom.

The precursors, or the starting molecules for these pathways, come primarily from the tryptophan metabolism. Tryptophan, an essential amino acid, undergoes various transformations, leading to the synthesis of psychedelic compounds. Interfering or modulating the levels of tryptophan in the mushrooms could offer new avenues to control the concentrations of the end products.

Beyond the primary and secondary metabolites, mushrooms likely produce a plethora of other molecules waiting to be discovered. These could range from protective antioxidants to compounds that interact with the known psychedelics, modulating their effects.

Individual Variability: The Kaleidoscope of Psychedelic Portraits

Just as artists mix colors to create diverse masterpieces, nature blends various compounds within mushroom strains, resulting in a spectrum of psychedelic experiences.

Detailed Exploration

Two mushroom strains might appear identical, yet their biochemical signatures could be worlds apart. The subtle interplay between psilocybin, psilocin, baeocystin, norbaeocystin, and even other yet-to-be-identified compounds can create a myriad of experiences. Some strains might induce profound visual hallucinations, while others could guide one toward emotional epiphanies.

Envision a future where choosing a mushroom strain becomes an art. With advanced knowledge, individuals could select strains as per their intent—be it for therapeutic healing, creative exploration, or spiritual quests. Akin to a sommelier recommending wine pairings, future psychedelic guides might suggest specific mushroom strains tailored to an individual's emotional and psychological landscape.

Individual responses to psychedelics are not solely based on the mushroom's chemical composition. Human genetic variations, especially in genes related to neurotransmitter function and metabolism, can also play a role. For instance, variations in the serotonin transporter gene might influence an individual's sensitivity or resistance to the effects of psilocybin.

Recent Research on Individual Variability: A study published in the "Journal of Psychopharmacology" in 2021 investigated the effects of genetic variability on the psilocybin experience. The researchers considered polymorphisms – variations in individual genes that could influence how the body reacts to drugs. They found that individuals with certain polymorphisms in the HTR2A gene – which codes for a specific serotonin receptor in the brain – reported different qualitative experiences after ingesting psilocybin. Specifically, those with a particular variant of the HTR2A gene described their trips as being more "mystical" and "insightful" compared to those without the variant.

Another important aspect is the role of the metabolism enzyme monoamine oxidase (MAO). This enzyme is responsible for breaking down neurotransmitters like serotonin, dopamine, and norepinephrine. Variations in genes related to MAO can influence its activity, potentially affecting the duration and intensity of a psychedelic experience. A study from the University of Zurich in 2020 suggested that individuals with a more active MAO enzyme had shorter and less intense psilocybin experiences.

These findings underscore the importance of considering genetics when studying the effects of psychedelics. They offer a glimpse into the complexity of the relationship between our genetic makeup and our experiences with substances like psilocybin.

As our understanding grows, the potential for "designer" mushrooms arises. Through selective breeding or genetic modification, it might be possible in the future to craft mushroom strains that have specific ratios of psychoactive compounds, offering more predictable and targeted experiences.

The dynamic interplay between mushrooms and their environment is not to be overlooked. Delving into the realm of mycorrhizal relationships reveals a deeper understanding of how mushrooms might be influenced externally. These symbiotic exchanges, where nature's equilibrium is maintained, could hold answers to the varying potencies and experiences offered by different mushroom strains. As researchers peer into this symbiosis, we might find that the key to understanding and potentially steering the psychedelic potential of a mushroom lies in the intricate embrace between fungi and flora.

A Dive into Mushroom Mycorrhizal Relationships

Mushrooms, including the psychedelic varieties, don't thrive in isolation. They form symbiotic relationships with plants, known as mycorrhizal associations. These relationships might indirectly influence the mushrooms' chemical compositions.

- **Nature's Network**: Mycorrhizal associations enable mushrooms to exchange nutrients with plants. In return for water and nutrients, the fungi provide the plants with sugars. This bi-directional exchange might affect the metabolic processes of the mushrooms, thereby influencing their chemical profiles.
- **Environment's Echo**: The type of plant a mushroom associates with, the soil chemistry, and the microbial community can all echo into the mushroom's chemical makeup. It's conceivable that these external factors, through the lens of mycorrhizal relationships, imprint upon the mushroom's psychedelic symphony.

Psychedelic mushrooms are more than their headline compounds. They're intricate chemical puzzles waiting to be pieced together. Recognizing the potential 'entourage effect' in mushrooms underscores the importance of holistic research, ensuring we appreciate and harness the full breadth of their therapeutic potential.

Comparing Psilocybin with Other Psychedelics

Psychedelics, a group of substances famed for their profound effects on perception, mood, and cognition, are diverse in their origins, structures, and effects. Among them, psilocybin, often extracted from specific mushroom species, has been the subject of much attention and scientific inquiry. Comparing it to other notable psychedelics, like DMT and LSD, can provide an illuminating overview of the world of mind-altering substances.

Chemical Structures: Delving into the Molecular Dance of Psychedelics

Like keys designed to fit into specific locks, the structures of psychedelic compounds are precisely fashioned to interact with our brain's receptors. The fundamental architecture of many psychedelics can be traced back to the tryptamine lineage, akin to the naturally occurring neurotransmitter serotonin.

Deep Dive

The name 'tryptamine' might sound technical, but it's the very backbone that many revered psychedelics are constructed upon. Just as members of a family share distinct facial features, psilocybin and DMT exhibit a structural kinship, both stemming from the tryptamine family tree. Similarly, LSD, while having a more intricate design, bears its roots in the tryptamine heritage.

Think of each psychedelic molecule as a classical music piece. While all might belong to the same genre, it's the minor variations and nuances in notes (or, in this case, molecular groups) that render each piece unique. This molecular distinctiveness intricately dictates how these compounds entwine with brain receptors, leading to diverse symphonies of experiences.

It's fascinating how slight variations in the chemical structure of a molecule can radically alter its interaction with receptors in the brain. Serotonin receptors, specifically the 5-HT2A receptor subtype, are primary targets for many psychedelics. The way each molecule fits into this receptor, like a hand fitting into a glove, determines the intensity and quality of its effect.

At the heart of many psychedelics is the indole ring, a specific molecular structure found in both tryptamines and serotonin. This commonality underpins why many of these compounds can interact with serotonin receptors in the first place.

While the tryptamine family has given us a rich tapestry of compounds, it's essential not to overlook the phenethylamine family. Mescaline, derived from cacti like Peyote and San Pedro, is a primary member of this group. While it shares the same basic aromatic ring structure with tryptamines, its side chain and overall molecular arrangement differ, leading to unique interactions within the brain and a distinct set of experiences for its users.

Different Effects & Durations: Navigating the Vast Psychedelic Seascape

Sailors venturing onto the high seas know that each voyage promises unique vistas and challenges. Similarly, embarking on a psychedelic journey, depending on the molecular ship one chooses, can vary in its duration and visual tapestry.

Detailed Exploration

- **The Long Waltz with LSD**: LSD, often hailed as the grandmaster of psychedelics, offers a marathon of cognitive ballet. The way LSD snugly fits into serotonin receptors, almost getting trapped within, prolongs its effects, leading to extensive trips that can dance through an entire day or night.

- **Psilocybin's Temporal Voyage**: Psilocybin, on the other hand, orchestrates a moderate-length ballet. After ingestion, it's swiftly transformed into psilocin, which serenades the brain with visions and introspections. However, this dance, though profound, wraps up in a shorter timeframe, typically ebbing away after a few hours.

- **Ayahuasca and DMT's Prolonged Interaction:** DMT on its own is typically short-acting, but when taken as a brew like Ayahuasca (combined with other plants containing MAOIs), the experience is extended. The MAOI prevents DMT from being rapidly broken down in the gut and liver, allowing for a longer and more profound journey.

Beyond the primary effects, many users report an "afterglow" phase post-trip, where they feel a sense of renewed purpose, clarity, or enhanced mood. This phase can vary in duration based on the psychedelic used and individual factors.

- **Salvia divinorum**, often just called Salvia, provides a unique psychedelic experience. Its active compound, salvinorin A, is neither a tryptamine nor a phenethylamine. Instead, it belongs to a class called diterpenoids. Unlike the others, Salvia primarily affects the kappa opioid receptors, leading to profoundly dissociative and atypical psychedelic effects. While its journey is intense, it's remarkably short-lived, often culminating within a few minutes to an hour.

Safety Profile: The Guiding Star in Therapeutic Horizons

In the galaxy of psychedelics, not all stars shine with the same intensity of safety. While some are embraced for their benign nature, others come with cautionary tales.

Elaborate Insights

- **Psilocybin's Legacy of Safety**: Tracing back through the annals of history, indigenous cultures revered and utilized psilocybin mushrooms in sacred rituals. This millennia-old bond stands as a

testament to psilocybin's safety. Modern scientific inquiries further echo this sentiment, highlighting its minimal addiction potential and toxicity.
- **Contrasting Companions**: Venturing into the realms of LSD and DMT, the narrative slightly shifts. LSD, owing to its prolonged trips, might heighten the risk of adverse psychological episodes, especially if one isn't in a conducive environment. DMT, bursting forth with intense visual and auditory cascades, demands mental preparation; without it, one might find oneself overwhelmed, akin to a sailor facing a sudden tempest.
- **Setting and Supervision**: One of the critical factors contributing to the safety profile of any psychedelic is the context in which it's consumed. Clinical studies often underscore the importance of a controlled setting with trained supervisors or therapists to guide the journey, mitigating potential negative outcomes.
- **Physical vs. Psychological Safety**: It's worth differentiating between these two. Physiologically, most classic psychedelics have a high safety margin, meaning the dose required for therapeutic effects is much lower than a dose that might cause harm. However, psychologically, unprepared or vulnerable individuals might experience distressing or challenging trips, emphasizing the importance of mental preparedness and proper setting.
- **Potential Interactions**: As with all compounds, there's a need to be wary of interactions with other substances, both legal and illicit. For instance, combining SSRIs (common antidepressants) with psychedelics can attenuate the effects of the latter or lead to a rare but serious condition called serotonin syndrome.
- **Tolerance Build-Up**: One remarkable feature of classic psychedelics like psilocybin, LSD, and DMT is the rapid development of tolerance. After an intense psychedelic experience, consuming the same dose shortly after will usually result in a diminished effect. This natural check-and-balance mechanism often discourages daily use and potential abuse. Interestingly, this tolerance can extend cross-substance; for instance, using LSD one day might reduce the effects of psilocybin the next. However, this tolerance usually resets after a week or so of abstinence.

In essence, psilocybin stands as a distinct entity in the vast universe of psychedelics. While sharing threads of similarity with other substances, its unique safety profile and moderate duration make it an intriguing candidate for therapeutic applications. As with all psychedelics, understanding, respect, and careful use are key.

Conclusion

The journey of psilocybin through the human body is a remarkable tale of biochemical transformations. Its passage from ingestion to psychoactive experience involves an intricate molecular dance. Psilocybin's conversion to psilocin, facilitated by the liver's diligent enzymatic processes, unlocks its mind-altering potential. Without this crucial step, the doors to the mystical psychedelic realm would remain closed.

Beyond this key reaction, the symphony of interactions between psilocybin-derived compounds and the brain's receptors choreographs a multidimensional experience. The subjective effects induced are paralleled by equally fascinating modulations in neural connectivity and activity. Modern imaging techniques have illuminated these changes, bridging subjective accounts with objective data.

While psilocybin takes center stage, a supporting cast of molecules contributes to the entourage effect, fine-tuning the overall experience. Aeruginascin, baeocystin, norbaeocystin - these obscure compounds hint at the untapped complexity within psychedelic fungi.

As research continues to unravel the mysteries of psilocybin's passage through body and mind, it becomes evident that pharmacology and mysticism need not be disparate domains. The clinical data being garnered is more than just scientific literature; it is the modern syntax illuminating an ancient language that has long conveyed healing, knowledge, and an unbridled understanding of consciousness itself.

CHAPTER 3: The Origins and History of Psilocybin Mushrooms

Ancient cultures have used psilocybin mushrooms in religious and spiritual ceremonies for thousands of years.

- Ancient civilizations and their usage
- The discovery and study in the Western world
- Legal battles and classifications

Psilocybin mushrooms, colloquially known as "magic mushrooms," have been intertwined with the cultural fabric of several ancient civilizations.

Sumerians and Babylonians

The ancient Sumerian and Babylonian civilizations flourished in the Mesopotamian region, which is modern-day southern Iraq. These cultures were the bedrock for many foundational aspects of human civilization. The Sumerians, in particular, are credited with the creation of cuneiform writing on clay tablets, which became a significant medium for documenting knowledge, religious practices, and legal matters. The Babylonians, on the other hand, are renowned for the Hammurabi Code, one of the earliest sets of legal rules. Their architectures, especially the famed ziggurats, stood as monumental testaments to their achievements in urban planning and construction.

Mushrooms had a distinctive presence in the art forms of both Sumerians and Babylonians. These motifs can be seen depicted in their sculptures, carvings, and even in the illustrations on clay tablets. The consistent association of mushroom symbols with religious ceremonies and spiritual realms is particularly intriguing. This gives rise to the speculation about mushrooms, particularly those with psychoactive properties, being used in rituals and sacred practices.

In many ancient cultures, the mushroom's unique life cycle and growth patterns, emerging overnight and withering rapidly, were often equated with themes of rebirth, regeneration, and connection to the divine. The mushroom's umbrella-like cap might have also been interpreted as a symbol of protection and shelter.

Entheogens are substances taken in a religious context to induce alterations in perception, mood, and various cognitive processes. In the Sumerian and Babylonian context, if psilocybin mushrooms were used, they would likely fit this category, serving as a conduit between the human and divine realms.

Certain ancient hymns and texts written in cuneiform make mention of a mysterious "plant of immortality." While the precise identity of this plant remains debated among scholars, there is a compelling argument that this could refer to psilocybin mushrooms. The concept of immortality or transcendence is often linked with altered states of consciousness, which is a hallmark effect of consuming psychedelic mushrooms.

Their references to such a plant might be an indication of their search for substances that provide elevation from mundane reality. Given the transformative experiences that psilocybin mushrooms induce, it is conceivable that they might have been seeking out such substances to understand or perhaps even attempt to transcend the human experience.

The Sumerians and Babylonians had a rich pantheon of gods and goddesses, each with its unique lore and ceremonies. These religious practices were deeply rooted in nature and the cosmos. The presence of mushroom motifs in their religious contexts hints at the possibility that mushrooms played a role in these ceremonies. They might have been used as sacraments to foster communion with the deities or perhaps as a tool to aid shamans and priests in their spiritual journeys and divination.

While concrete evidence about the Sumerian and Babylonian use of psilocybin mushrooms is sparse, the recurring mushroom motifs in their art and references in their hymns cannot be overlooked. They underscore the potential importance of mushrooms, possibly as sacred tools for spiritual exploration, in these ancient cultures.

Greeks

Ancient Greece, spanning the period from the 8th century BC to the fall of the Roman Empire in 476 AD, was a civilization of unparalleled achievements. It laid down the foundation for Western philosophy, arts, drama, and the sciences. Moreover, its myriad city-states, each with its own culture and practices, contributed to a tapestry of religious and spiritual rites that have intrigued historians for centuries.

Philosophers like Socrates, Plato, and Aristotle often pondered the nature of reality, consciousness, and the human soul. Their quest for understanding might have intersected with the use of substances that altered perception, allowing for deeper introspection.

The Eleusinian Mysteries, centered in the city of Eleusis, stand out as one of the most secretive and revered religious rites of ancient Greece. They were held annually and were dedicated to the goddesses Demeter and Persephone. For nearly two millennia, these rites were attended by thousands, from humble farmers to esteemed statesmen like Plato and Cicero.

The strict code of silence (or "hierospygia") maintained by the initiates has made it challenging for historians to unearth the precise nature of the ceremonies. However, this veil of secrecy added to the allure of the rites, making them even more sought-after.

Central to the Eleusinian Mysteries was the consumption of a special potion known as "kykeon." Ancient records, especially those from the likes of Homer in his work 'The Iliad', describe kykeon as a concoction made from barley, water, and certain herbs. The precise nature and properties of these herbs have been a matter of great debate. While there's no direct reference to psilocybin mushrooms, the transformative experiences reported by the initiates post-consumption have led some scholars to theorize that kykeon might have contained psychoactive substances. The inclusion of such substances would help explain the profound spiritual revelations and visions experienced during the ceremonies.

The Eleusinian Mysteries were deeply embedded in the poignant myth of Persephone, the daughter of the grain goddess Demeter. Persephone's abduction by Hades, the god of the underworld, and the subsequent grief of Demeter formed the thematic essence of these rituals. The initiates would re-enact this myth, symbolizing the cyclical nature of life, death, and rebirth. The consumption of kykeon and the subsequent experiences can be viewed as a symbolic journey to the underworld and back, mirroring Persephone's own journey.

Given the profound, life-altering experiences reported by those initiated into the Eleusinian Mysteries, it's plausible to hypothesize the use of entheogens like psilocybin mushrooms. These substances have been known to induce experiences of ego dissolution, unity with the universe, and profound spiritual insights – all of which align with the descriptions of the mysteries.

Beyond the Eleusinian Mysteries, there are other instances hinting at the Greeks' familiarity with mind-altering substances. The "Oracle of Delphi" is another example where priestesses, known as Pythias, would enter trance-like states, possibly facilitated by intoxicating vapors or substances, to offer prophecies.

Historians like Herodotus have documented the use of various substances by neighboring cultures. Such cross-cultural exchanges might have introduced the Greeks to various entheogens, influencing their religious practices.

While the true nature of the Eleusinian Mysteries and the exact composition of kykeon remain speculative, the potential role of psychoactive substances, possibly derived from mushrooms, offers a captivating lens through which to view these ancient rites. Such a perspective bridges the chasm between the ancient and the modern, hinting at the timeless human quest for spiritual transcendence.

Mayans and Aztecs: Ceremonial Rituals

The sophisticated civilizations of the Mayans and Aztecs were deeply intertwined with nature, weaving a tapestry of spirituality, astronomy, and botanical wisdom. Central to this were the revered psilocybin mushrooms, seen as sacred keys to the cosmos.

Ceremonial Significance

In the worldview of the ancient Mayans and Aztecs, psilocybin mushrooms were regarded with immense reverence. Unlike other substances consumed for nourishment or pleasure, these mushrooms were considered tools of spiritual enlightenment. Their use was demarcated from the mundane and every day; they were not substances one would encounter in casual settings or consume impulsively.

Psilocybin mushrooms were often consumed during significant calendrical events. The intricate Mayan and Aztec calendars, which tracked both solar and lunar cycles, pinpointed special days when the veil between the physical and spiritual worlds was believed to be thinnest. On these days, mushrooms were used as a conduit to access other realms.

The manner of preparing and consuming the mushrooms was ritualistic. They might be blended with honey, cocoa, or other sacred substances, and prayers or chants would be recited as they were ingested. These preparations and rites ensured the experience was rooted in sacredness.

Historical records, including writings from Spanish conquistadors and Catholic missionaries, often point to the deep respect Mesoamerican cultures had for these mushrooms. They noted the intentional and deliberate manner in which the mushrooms were consumed, always with a larger spiritual or communal purpose in mind.

The act of offering psilocybin mushrooms to the gods was a common practice. Ceremonial altars have been discovered, adorned with intricate carvings of mushroom motifs. These altars often served as spaces where mushrooms were placed as offerings before being consumed by the attendees of the ritual.

The Mayans and Aztecs believed that the mushrooms were gifts from the gods. They were seen as a medium to connect with the divine, ensuring that the consumers approached them with utmost respect. Unlike other substances, there was a deep-seated belief in their transformative power, a belief rooted in generations of tradition.

Priests or shamans often facilitated these ceremonies. As spiritual intermediaries, they would guide participants through their journeys, ensuring safe and meaningful experiences. Their roles were crucial, as they would interpret the visions or messages received during the trance states.

Not just any location was deemed appropriate for these ceremonies. Sacred caves, temples, or specific clearings in forests were chosen. These spaces were believed to be charged with spiritual energy, enhancing the mushroom-induced experiences.

While several mushroom varieties grew in Mesoamerica, not all were deemed sacred. Only specific types, recognized for their potent visionary properties, were revered and used in ceremonies.

There might have been specific times in the year, perhaps aligned with the agricultural or lunar calendar, when the consumption of these mushrooms was considered most auspicious.

Some of the indigenous Mesoamerican codices (ancient illustrated manuscripts) might hint at the sacred use of mushrooms. While many codices were destroyed by the Spanish, those that remain provide valuable insights into the spiritual practices of the Mayans and Aztecs.

Mushroom Stones: Archaeologists have unearthed mushroom-shaped stones from various Mesoamerican sites. These stones, dating back to as early as 3000 B.C., might represent the ancient and continuous reverence for the sacred mushroom.

Mushroom Deities: Some historians speculate that there were specific deities associated with mushrooms. These deities might have been invoked during ceremonies to bless the participants and ensure a fruitful journey into the spiritual realm.

Significant life events, such as births, deaths, or transitions into adulthood, were often accompanied by the consumption of these sacred fungi. They were used as tools to seek guidance, blessings, or insights as individuals transition from one phase of life to another.

As adolescents transition to adulthood, they might undertake a vision quest facilitated by the mushrooms. These quests were rites of passage, and the insights gained during the experience would guide the individual in their adult life.

In the context of death and the afterlife, mushrooms might have been consumed to communicate with ancestors or to guide the spirit of the deceased to the next realm.

Beyond individual experiences, these rituals also served as communal bonding exercises. Shared visions or experiences under the influence of psilocybin mushrooms forged a deeper sense of unity and understanding within communities. Stories and insights gained during these communal mushroom ceremonies would be passed down through generations. These oral traditions, enriched by shared experiences under the influence of psilocybin, formed an integral part of the cultural and spiritual fabric of the community.

Shamanic Journeys

In Mesoamerican cultures, shamans held a unique position. They were the spiritual guides, the connectors between the tangible and the ethereal. Using psilocybin mushrooms, they would embark on spiritual journeys, acting as conduits between the human and spirit realms.

Not everyone could become a shaman. There was often a rigorous process of selection, initiation, and training. Potential shamans underwent years of apprenticeship under experienced guides, learning not just about mushrooms but the entire spectrum of the spiritual world.

Historical accounts and tribal folklore are replete with tales of shamans diagnosing mysterious ailments, prophesying future events, or even providing solutions to community disputes while under the influence of these mushrooms. The vivid and symbolic nature of their visions was considered an unambiguous message from higher powers.

Apart from visions induced by mushrooms, shamans also placed significant emphasis on dreams. They believed that dreams were another realm of communication with the spirit world. Often, the symbols and lessons from these dreams would be used to interpret or enhance the mushroom-induced experiences.

While shamans were the primary consumers of psilocybin mushrooms, there were instances where others in the community might partake. However, this was never a solitary or impulsive endeavor. It was always undertaken under the supervision of a seasoned shaman, ensuring that the experience was both meaningful and safeguarded.

Ritualistic Practices

For ancient civilizations, the movements of celestial bodies were not just astronomical events but were deeply symbolic and spiritually significant. The cosmos was seen as a mirror reflecting the divine plan, and terrestrial events, especially spiritual ceremonies, were often synchronized with these celestial occurrences.

Examples

1. The Mayan civilization, renowned for their precise astronomical observations, might hold mushroom ceremonies during solar or lunar eclipses, viewing these as moments when the veils between different realms were at their thinnest.
2. During the winter solstice, when the sun was "reborn" after the longest night, some tribes consumed these mushrooms to gain insights and revelations for the year ahead.

Before any ritual commenced, a conducive environment was created. This could involve cleaning the area, creating protective circles with stones or herbs, or even drawing symbols that hold spiritual significance for the tribe or community.

Psilocybin mushrooms were not consumed in isolation. They were often combined with other sacred plants or herbs, believed to enhance or protect the spiritual journey.

Collective activities like chanting, singing, and dancing were not just expressions of joy or reverence; they were techniques to unify the energies of all participants. By synchronizing their rhythms and vibrations, a group could achieve a heightened collective consciousness, making the mushroom-induced journey more profound.

Instruments like drums, rattles, and flutes played a pivotal role. They were not just musical accompaniments but tools to navigate the spiritual realm. The rhythm of a drum, for instance, could guide the pace and intensity of a vision.

Examples

1. The Mazatec people of Mexico, known for their usage of sacred mushrooms, would often chant hymns, invoking spirits or deities before consuming the fungi.

2. In certain South American tribes, elaborate dances mimicking the growth and lifecycle of the mushroom might be performed, encapsulating the journey from Earth to enlightenment.

The act of harvesting psilocybin mushrooms wasn't a mundane agricultural task. It was a spiritual endeavor, with each step—from identifying the right mushrooms to picking them—imbued with ritualistic significance.

The phases of the moon, believed to influence the potency and spiritual essence of the mushrooms, played a pivotal role. New moons or full moons, being particularly powerful phases, were often chosen as ideal times for harvest.

Apart from moon phases, certain seasons or periods, especially post-rainfall, were believed to imbue the mushrooms with enhanced spiritual potency.

The first mushroom appearing after the first rains of the season was especially revered. Special rituals, which might include songs or dances of gratitude, were performed before harvesting this mushroom.

Before plucking a mushroom, a silent or vocal prayer of thanks might be offered to the Earth and the spirits. This gratitude ensured that the fungi's spiritual essence remained intact and that the balance of nature was preserved.

Examples

- The indigenous Shipibo-Conibo people, while primarily known for their use of Ayahuasca, demonstrate a deep reverence for all psychoactive plants. A similar respect would be paid to mushrooms, seeing them as sentient beings rather than mere plants.
- Among the Huichol tribes, before harvesting any sacred plant, offerings of corn, beads, or even small figurines might be left as a token of gratitude.

Transcendental Experiences

While modern science may classify these visions as hallucinations or altered perceptions, for ancient participants, they were very real and spiritually significant. The visions weren't arbitrary but often aligned with the cultural and spiritual beliefs of the individual or community.

Participants often felt a deep sense of interconnectedness with the cosmos. They didn't just feel like observers of the universe but an intrinsic part of it, leading to profound realizations about the nature of existence.

Examples

1. An Aztec priest might see Quetzalcoatl, the feathered serpent god, offering guidance or prophecies.//
2. A Mayan shaman might journey through the underworld, encountering spirits of past ancestors and reliving the tales of the Popol Vuh, their sacred book.
3. In other cultures, like the indigenous tribes of Australia, participants might encounter totemic animals or Dreamtime spirits, reaffirming their connection to the land and its lore.

While the spiritual and emotional effects are highlighted, participants also experienced physical effects. These could range from nausea to heightened sensitivity to light and sound. Shamans, aware of these effects, ensured that participants were in a safe environment and were given remedies if any adverse reactions occurred.

The release wasn't just emotional. It could manifest physically in the form of intense shaking, vocal expressions, or spontaneous movements, representing the freeing of suppressed energies.

This cathartic experience was therapeutic. By confronting and releasing suppressed emotions or traumatic memories, participants often found healing and liberation. In many ways, it mirrors what modern psychology aims to achieve through cathartic therapy.

Examples

1. Among the Mazatec community, a participant, upon confronting past grief, might wail or cry, releasing years of pent-up sorrow. The collective community would support this, seeing it as a process of cleansing and renewal.
2. In some Native American tribes, laughter during a ritual might symbolize the joy of reconnecting with one's inner child or the pure essence of existence.

These weren't fleeting realizations. Participants often spent days or even weeks integrating these insights into their daily lives, transforming not just their personal beliefs but sometimes even influencing the direction of the entire community.

Many participants, after their journeys, were inspired to create. This could manifest as intricate carvings, paintings, or even songs and stories that chronicled their experiences. Some of the art and crafts of Mesoamerican civilizations might have their roots in these psychedelic inspirations.

While many experiences were passed down orally, some were inscribed on stones, hides, or even in the form of glyphs. These records served as guides for future generations, providing insights into the spiritual beliefs and practices of the community.

Leaders or decision-makers in a tribe or community would often partake in these rituals before making significant decisions, seeking guidance and wisdom.

Examples

1. A chieftain, after a mushroom-induced journey, might realize the importance of forging an alliance with a neighboring tribe, having seen visions of unity and collaboration.

2. An individual feeling lost or purposeless might emerge from the experience with a newfound role, such as becoming a healer, artist, or storyteller, after receiving insights about their innate gifts and talents.

The Mayans and Aztecs did not see the mushrooms as mere tools but as sacred keys, unlocking realms of consciousness, wisdom, and divine guidance. These experiences, deeply ingrained in their rituals and practices, influenced not just individual lives but shaped the very foundations of their civilizations.

Xochipilli: The Divine Psychedelic Connection

The detailed depictions of Xochipilli not only showcase the importance of the deity in the cultural and spiritual life of the Aztecs but also the immense value they placed on the natural world.

His image often showcases him seated on a flower-covered throne, with mushrooms visible on his body, symbolizing the intertwined nature of the divine and the botanical kingdom.

The flowers adorning Xochipilli aren't random. They are carefully chosen, representing various plants with psychoactive properties, reinforcing the god's connection to altered states of consciousness.

Xochipilli wasn't just a deity of generic pleasure but was deeply intertwined with enthoegenic or spiritual experiences induced by plants and fungi.

Apart from mushrooms, other botanical elements associated with Xochipilli, like tobacco, morning glory, and cacao, all had ritualistic significance and were believed to possess transformative properties.

Those embarking on psychedelic expeditions often invoked Xochipilli as a guide, hoping for joyous and enlightening experiences under his benevolent watch.

Beyond ritualistic purposes, the plants and fungi associated with Xochipilli had a significant influence on daily Aztec life. Many were used as medicines, aphrodisiacs, and even currency in certain contexts.

Dance and music, in the Aztec worldview, were not just for entertainment. They were spiritual practices in themselves, mediums through which they could harmonize their inner energies with the rhythms of the cosmos.

Aztecs believed that celestial bodies influenced the potency of psychoactive plants. Xochipilli, being so deeply intertwined with these plants, had ceremonies that often aligned with specific celestial events.

During festivals dedicated to Xochipilli, the air would resonate with drums, flutes, and chants, with participants dancing in intricate patterns. These ceremonies were believed to invoke the god's spirit, blessing the community with harmony, creativity, and joy.

In rituals involving the consumption of sacred mushrooms, music and dance played pivotal roles in directing the experience. The entrancing rhythms would guide the participants' visions, making them more profound and insightful.

For the Aztecs, Xochipilli symbolized the harmonious synthesis of the sensory and the divine, the earthly and the celestial. The deity's association with both psychedelic substances and artistic expressions underscores the ancient belief in the interconnectedness of all forms of ecstatic experiences, be it through dance, song, or sacred mushrooms.

Sacred Botany

The very foundation of Xochipilli's temple carvings provides a visual lexicon of the enthoegenic plants and fungi revered in Aztec culture. Such iconographic details aren't mere artistic choices but are deliberate inclusions highlighting the deity's deep-rooted connection with sacred botany.

Given his portrayal alongside these powerful botanical symbols, Xochipilli was perceived as a protector of the rituals that revolved around these substances. He was invoked to ensure that these ceremonies remained pure, that the substances were respected and not misused, and that participants had meaningful and safe experiences.

The intricate carvings served as a tangible guide to the initiated, signifying which plants and fungi were suitable for spiritual exploration and which ones were taboo or reserved for specific ceremonies.

While Xochipilli was the primary deity associated with sacred botany, other Aztec gods and goddesses were invoked during rituals involving entheogens, forming a pantheon of interconnected divine entities.

Symbol of Altered Consciousness

Xochipilli's association with psychoactive substances wasn't limited to their physical effects. Instead, it was deeply symbolic of the spiritual portals these substances could open. Ingesting them wasn't just about experiencing hallucinations; it was about transcending the mortal realm to gain insights from the divine or ancestral spirits.

Those who partook in the ceremonies believed that, under the watchful eyes of Xochipilli, they could confront their innermost fears, desires, and aspirations, undergoing a transformative introspection that would redefine their place in the cosmos.

Apart from spiritual journeys, Xochipilli was also invoked in healing ceremonies. Sacred plants were used to treat both physical ailments and spiritual afflictions, with the deity acting as the bridge between the tangible and intangible realms.

Xochipilli's imagery, coupled with his associations, encapsulates the harmonization of opposing forces. The euphoria and the fear, the known and the unknown, the mortal and the immortal. His presence in rituals was a reminder of the delicate balance between pleasure and reverence, between enjoying the sensory delights and acknowledging the profound spiritual implications of the journey.

The significance of Xochipilli and his entheogenic associations highlights a sophisticated understanding of consciousness within Aztec culture. It underscores the value they placed on exploring alternate states of mind, not for mere recreation, but as a crucial aspect of spiritual growth and community bonding.

Feasts and Festivals

Events dedicated to Xochipilli weren't merely about individual experiences. They were community-driven, turning into massive celebrations where entire groups would participate, feeling united in their ecstatic states. This not only honored Xochipilli but also solidified communal bonds.

During these feasts, unique instruments would be played, many of which resonated with the rhythmic beats of nature, mimicking the chirping of birds or the rustling of leaves. Such music enhanced the psychoactive-induced experiences, guiding the participants through auditory landscapes.

Foods prepared during these feasts weren't just sustenance. Many dishes were carefully curated to complement the effects of the consumed substances, often using herbs and spices believed to enhance visions or ground participants during intense experiences.

After consuming entheogens, participants would often sleep within the temple grounds. Dreams were believed to be an essential medium of communication with Xochipilli, and recounting dreams was an integral part of post-ceremony discussions.

Sacred Spaces

The temples of Xochipilli were masterpieces designed in a way to amplify the psychoactive journeys. With labyrinthine corridors and chambers illuminated by the soft glow of torches, the architectural design itself could lead one into a trance.

Many of these temples were strategically located near natural settings like forests, gardens, or water bodies. The presence of nature intensified the experiences, with participants feeling more connected to the world around them.

Many of Xochipilli's temples were aligned with astronomical phenomena. The positioning was believed to amplify the effects of the consumed entheogens and enhance communication with celestial beings.

Burnt incense and fragrant flowers filled these sanctuaries, their scents mingling with the air, adding an olfactory dimension to the spiritual journey. Specific fragrances were chosen for their properties to calm, invigorate, or enhance visions.

Prayers and Offerings

Prayers to Xochipilli were often rhythmic, sometimes resembling poetic verses. They were meant to tune the mind and prepare the soul for the experience ahead, acting as a bridge between the mundane and the mystical.

Apart from verbal prayers, offerings like flowers, fruits, or even small sculptures were presented at the deity's altar. These tangible tokens were symbolic gestures of gratitude, love, and respect.

The altars dedicated to Xochipilli often incorporated sacred geometries, believed to be patterns of creation. Offerings were placed in these patterns to align with the cosmic energies and optimize the ceremonial outcomes.

For those not well-versed in prayers, temple priests or shamans would often lead group meditations before the consumption of entheogens. This ritual not only invoked Xochipilli's blessings but also centered the participants, ensuring they approached the journey with the right mindset.

Lasting Influence

Despite the passage of time and cultural amalgamations, indigenous tribes in Mexico, such as the Huichol and the Mazatecs, still maintain age-old traditions where they invoke deities akin to Xochipilli during their sacred ceremonies. These traditions have persisted, resisting colonial pressures and modern-day secularism.

For these communities, Xochipilli isn't just a figure from ancient tales; he's a living entity guarding the sanctity of nature and its many gifts. This relationship strengthens their bond with the environment and their understanding of sustainable practices.

Recognizing the importance of the plants sacred to Xochipilli, the Aztecs developed advanced agricultural techniques to cultivate them. This legacy can still be seen in certain indigenous farming methods in Mexico.

Modern Psychedelic Renaissance

Contemporary research, especially in institutions like Johns Hopkins University and Imperial College London, has begun to acknowledge the therapeutic potential of psychedelics. As these substances become decriminalized in various parts of the world, Xochipilli's iconography serves as a reminder of their ancient and sacred origins.

Modern therapists, especially those involved in psychedelic-assisted therapies, often use symbols, narratives, or even mantras from ancient cultures, including those related to Xochipilli, to help guide and anchor patients during their therapeutic sessions.

Contemporary neo shamanic practices, particularly in the Western world, have been significantly influenced by the rituals associated with Xochipilli. This has given rise to hybrid ceremonies that combine indigenous traditions with modern spiritual movements.

Artistic Representations

Murals, paintings, and sculptures showcasing Xochipilli can be seen not only in museums but also in contemporary art galleries, where artists reinterpret his imagery to resonate with modern audiences. These pieces often incorporate vibrant colors, intricate patterns, and juxtapositions of the ancient with the modern.

Bands, especially those in the psychedelic rock or trance genres, have used motifs associated with Xochipilli in their album art, lyrics, and stage setups. These sonic and visual experiences transport audiences, echoing the very essence of what Xochipilli represented.

Xochipilli's vivid imagery has been adapted into fashion, with motifs appearing on clothing, jewelry, and even tattoos. This adaptation reflects a broader cultural recognition of Xochipilli beyond just art and music.

Poets and authors, inspired by the lore of Xochipilli, have woven tales that revolve around psychedelic journeys, transformative experiences, and the interplay between man, nature, and the divine.

The profound reverence for Xochipilli, both in history and contemporary times, underscores humanity's enduring relationship with the enigmatic world of psychedelics. It showcases how an ancient deity can bridge the gap between past and present, reminding us of the sacredness inherent in nature and our profound connection to it.

Indigenous Tribes: Shamanistic Practices

Various tribes across the globe utilized these mushrooms for spiritual guidance.

Siberia: Communing with the Spirit World

The Amanita muscaria (Fly Agaric), with its distinct red cap and white spots, has been featured in numerous myths and legends worldwide. In Siberia, its psychedelic properties became central to spiritual practices, especially among shamans.

Beyond its immediate region, the knowledge of the Amanita muscaria's properties spread to other parts of Eurasia. This happened due to trade routes and migrations. Some even theorize that the mushroom's famous presence in European folklore, like the tales of "fairy circles," might be influenced by Siberian knowledge.

Consumption of the fly agaric produces vivid hallucinations, along with sensations of flying or floating. This experience further reinforced the belief that shamans could physically travel between realms.

Shamanic Journeys: Navigating the Ethereal Landscape

Before the ingestion of these mushrooms, shamans often underwent elaborate purification rituals. These could involve fasting, sweating ceremonies (similar to saunas), and specific chants to prepare their spirit for the journey ahead.

Siberian cosmology often speaks of multiple layers of existence - the underworld, middle Earth, and the heavens. With the aid of the Amanita muscaria, shamans claimed to navigate these planes, meeting various entities along the way.

Upon returning from their trance, shamans would interpret their visions, translating them into actionable advice for their tribes. For instance, a vision of a prosperous hunt could lead to tribal preparations for the same.

In the unforgiving Siberian landscapes, predicting weather was a vital survival skill. Some shamans claimed to foresee changes in weather patterns during their trances, guiding the tribe in their activities.

If a member of the community was ill, shamans would often conduct special ceremonies, using both the insights from their visions and other herbal remedies to restore the individual's health.

Apart from the mushrooms, Siberian shamans employed a range of instruments, like the drum (tungur), which they believed could help induce trance states or call upon spirits. The rhythmic beating of the drum was said to mimic the heartbeat, and it played a pivotal role in shamanic journeys.

Cultural Significance: A Legacy of Reverence

Siberian folklore is replete with tales of magical mushrooms, heroic shamans, and their epic journeys to the spirit realm. Over generations, these stories served both as entertainment and moral guidance, reflecting societal values and norms.

Presenting the Amanita muscaria as an offering wasn't just a sign of respect but also an acknowledgment of the mutual relationship between the shaman and the community. While the shaman provided guidance, the community ensured he/she was equipped for the ethereal journey.

The very appearance of the fly agaric mushroom often symbolized enlightenment, transformation, and the cyclical nature of life and death in Siberian art and craft.

Interestingly, reindeer in Siberia are known to seek out and consume fly agaric mushrooms. Some tribes observed the effects of the mushrooms on reindeer, which might have led to their own experiments with the fungus. Moreover, the relationship between the reindeer and the mushroom adds another layer of cultural and ecological significance.

In essence, the shamanistic practices of Siberia, centered around the Amanita muscaria, offer a fascinating insight into how indigenous cultures harnessed the power of nature to understand their place in the cosmos, guiding their communities with wisdom gleaned from their spiritual explorations.

Native Americans: Sacred Fungi of the New World

Different tribes had specific names and mythologies associated with these mushrooms. For example, the Nahuatl-speaking indigenous people of Mexico referred to psilocybin mushrooms as "teonanácatl," meaning "flesh of the gods."

Tales of gods gifting these mushrooms to humans as a means of enlightenment or as tools to bridge the earthly and divine realms were passed down through generations, either as oral narratives or in some forms of codices before European influence.

Not all "flesh of the gods" were equal. Depending on region, season, and specific mushroom species, the potency and resulting experiences could vary widely. This variability often led tribes to develop specialized techniques for mushroom cultivation or harvesting, ensuring that the most potent specimens were used for spiritual ceremonies.

Ritualistic Consumption: A Deep Spiritual Experience

Similar to other indigenous practices globally, before ingesting the mushrooms, participants often underwent cleansing rituals. These could involve fasting, purification by smoke, or the use of other sacred plants.

While shamans or spiritual leaders led these ceremonies, other members of the tribe would often join in collective prayers, songs, and dances. The objective was to form a spiritual synergy, uniting the community in their quest for divine connection.

For some tribes, especially in the Mesoamerican region, the phase of the moon played a significant role. Mushrooms were often harvested during specific moon phases, believing that this timing endowed them with enhanced spiritual properties.

By communicating with the 'spirit' of the mushrooms, individuals felt they could also connect with their ancestors, drawing on ancient wisdom and receiving guidance for current challenges.

The experiences induced by the mushrooms weren't just hallucinogenic escapades. They often provided deep introspection, helping individuals understand their life's purpose, rectify past mistakes, or fortify their role within the community.

While modern psychedelic enthusiasts often discuss the importance of "set" (mindset) and "setting" (environment) during psychedelic experiences, this concept was not new to indigenous tribes. The rituals, chants, and communal participation all contributed to a controlled set and setting, ensuring that the consumer of the mushrooms was in the right frame of mind and in an environment conducive to spiritual experiences.

Continued Legacy: Reclaiming Ancestral Wisdom

The European colonizers, particularly the Spanish in Mexico and other parts of Central America, viewed these practices as 'pagan' rituals. Consequently, they often suppressed or demonized the use of psilocybin mushrooms, pushing these traditions underground.

With the global resurgence of interest in psychedelics for mental health and spiritual growth, many Native American communities are actively working to reintroduce and preserve these ancient practices. This resurgence goes beyond just consumption, emphasizing the need for respect, proper ritualistic contexts, and understanding the mushrooms' sacred nature.

In the modern era, various Native American tribes have had to fight for their rights to practice traditional ceremonies involving the use of psilocybin mushrooms and other sacred plants. Landmark legal cases have emphasized religious freedom, leading to some protections for indigenous psychedelic practices.

From the vast plains of North America to the dense forests of Siberia, the reverence for mushrooms as sacred and transformative entities forms a universal thread. It's a testament to the innate human desire for connection, understanding, and transcendence. These age-old practices remind us of the deep bond between nature and humanity, emphasizing that true wisdom often lies in the harmonious integration of the two.

The Discovery and Study in the Western World

The allure of the mystical East and the ancient wisdom of indigenous cultures has, for centuries, captivated the Western mind. This fascination reached a pivotal juncture in the 20th century when the Western world was formally introduced to psilocybin mushrooms. Though these fungi had been used for millennia in traditional contexts, they now beckoned as a new frontier in both scientific research and countercultural exploration. This surge of interest in 'magic mushrooms' was initiated by individuals like Gordon Wasson, and soon, what started as a cultural discovery translated into groundbreaking scientific inquiries.

Gordon Wasson: Bridging Cultures Through Fungi

R. Gordon Wasson, initially a banker by profession, developed an intense passion for mycology - the study of fungi. This interest was heightened when he realized the stark contrast between the Western aversion to mushrooms and the reverence they held in other cultures.

Gordon Wasson's journey into the world of mycology was partly sparked by personal experiences. An anecdote suggests that his intrigue began when his Russian wife, Valentina, excitedly collected wild mushrooms during a walk in the woods, whereas he, with his Western upbringing, was suspicious of them. This stark contrast in attitudes towards fungi became a pivotal moment, setting the stage for his life's work.

Gordon wasn't the only one with an interest in ethnobotany; his wife, Valentina, also shared the passion. Together, they co-authored the book "Mushrooms, Russia, and History", a testament to their shared fascination.

Wasson didn't limit himself to academic study. He traveled extensively, diving deep into diverse cultures to understand their relationship with mushrooms. He realized that while many Western societies considered mushrooms with skepticism or even fear, numerous ancient cultures revered them for their culinary, medicinal, and spiritual properties.

Expedition to Mexico: A Voyage of Discovery

To ensure a comprehensive understanding, Wasson often collaborated with other experts during his trips. For his Mexican expedition, he was joined by Roger Heim, a renowned French mycologist, who helped identify and classify the mushrooms they encountered.

Their encounter with Maria Sabina, the Mazatec shamaness, wasn't just a casual introduction. Wasson and his wife developed a deep respect for her, understanding her pivotal role in preserving and transmitting the ancient Mazatec traditions. Sabina, despite initial reservations, agreed to let them participate in the velada, sharing her sacred knowledge.

Wasson not only focused on the mushrooms but also endeavored to understand the linguistic and cultural nuances of the Mazatec people. This holistic approach helped in fostering trust and understanding during their interactions.

The Transformative Velada Experience

The velada wasn't merely a recreational event. It was a deeply spiritual ceremony aiming to heal, offer guidance, or connect with the divine. The room was often adorned with Catholic icons, integrating indigenous beliefs with Christian symbolism, reflecting the syncretism of post-colonial Mazatec culture.

The use of Catholic icons in velada ceremonies showcases how indigenous practices adapted and survived despite Spanish colonization. This blending of belief systems made the ceremonies accessible to both indigenous Mazatecs and those of Spanish descent.

Wasson's experience was profound. He described vivid visions, a deep sense of interconnectedness, and a transcendence beyond the mundane. This direct experience with the 'magic' of these mushrooms solidified his commitment to studying and preserving such traditions.

Life Magazine: Introducing Psilocybin to the West

The Life magazine article was groundbreaking. It was one of the first mainstream introductions to psilocybin mushrooms, and its vivid descriptions captured the imagination of many in the West. Readers were fascinated, and soon, the 1960s saw a surge of individuals traveling to Mexico, seeking their own mushroom experiences.

Wasson's account wasn't just a cultural sensation; it piqued scientific curiosity. Notable figures like Dr. Timothy Leary were inspired to commence their own research on psychedelics. The Swiss chemist Albert Hofmann, who had previously synthesized LSD, collaborated with Wasson and Heim to isolate and identify the active compound in the mushrooms, naming it psilocybin.

R. Gordon Wasson's contributions transcended mere ethnobotanical exploration. By bridging the gap between ancient traditions and modern society, he facilitated a cross-cultural exchange, allowing the West to rediscover the ancient wisdom encapsulated in these sacred fungi. His journey highlights the beauty of interdisciplinary exploration, where passion, curiosity, and respect can lead to profound understanding and appreciation.

Research Flourishes: A New Frontier in Science

The resonance of Wasson's accounts in Life magazine extended beyond just curious readers and adventure seekers. It triggered a genuine intrigue in the scientific community, as many began to question how this natural substance could elicit such profound experiences.

While psychologists and psychiatrists naturally gravitated toward the potential applications of psilocybin, the compound also drew the attention of neuroscientists, chemists, and even cultural anthropologists, showcasing the multifaceted potential of the fungi.

Chemists were also drawn to understand the precise molecular structures of the compounds within these mushrooms. Their work laid the foundation for understanding the biochemical pathways by which psilocybin affects human consciousness.

Pioneering Studies: Trailblazers in Uncharted Waters

Dr. Timothy Leary and Dr. Richard Alpert's endeavors at Harvard were pioneering. They initiated the Harvard Psilocybin Project in 1960, aiming to study the effects of psilocybin on human consciousness, behavior, and societal structures. Their experiments included giving psilocybin to inmates to see if it reduced recidivism and the famous Marsh Chapel experiment, which analyzed its effects on religious experience.

However, their unorthodox methods, combined with growing societal concerns about psychedelics, led to the termination of the project in 1963. Despite the controversies, their work was seminal in planting the idea that psychedelics could have therapeutic value.

Leary and Alpert's research also hinted at the importance of "set and setting" in determining the outcome of a psychedelic experience. This concept highlighted the influence of one's mindset and the physical and social environment on the nature of the trip, a principle still fundamental in modern therapeutic uses of psychedelics.

Therapeutic Applications: From Anecdotal to Empirical

Clinical trials and studies over the years began revealing the mushrooms' potential to address various mental health challenges. For instance, research has indicated that psilocybin can help in creating lasting positive changes in mood, attitude, and behavior, especially when combined with psychotherapy.

The journey of psilocybin research in the Western world is a narrative of perseverance, curiosity, and rediscovery. It reflects humanity's innate desire to understand the self and the universe. As we continue to delve into the mysteries of psychedelics, we stand on the cusp of integrating age-old wisdom with cutting-edge science, promising better mental health outcomes and deeper insights into the human experience.

Early Scientific Explorations

The mid-20th century witnessed a paradigm shift in the world of psychoactive substances. As cultures merged and new compounds were discovered, the 1950s and 60s emerged as a watershed era for psilocybin mushrooms. The West, having been captivated by the ancient practices of indigenous tribes, was now eager to decipher the scientific secrets these fungi held. This period of exploration, led by luminaries like Albert Hofmann, was crucial not just for understanding the mushrooms but also for illuminating their potential therapeutic applications.

Albert Hofmann: Deciphering the Mushroom's Magic

While Albert Hofmann is most famously known for his accidental discovery of LSD's effects, his broader interest lies in understanding the chemical constituents of plants and fungi with cultural or medicinal significance. This passion led him to delve into the mysteries of psilocybin mushrooms, which had been used ceremonially by indigenous communities for centuries.

Hofmann's foray into the world of 'magic mushrooms' was directly influenced by R. Gordon Wasson's accounts. After learning about Wasson's experiences with the Mazatec shamans, Hofmann became keenly interested in isolating the active compound in these mushrooms.

Hofmann's efforts in isolating psilocybin were supported by his collaboration with the French mycologist Roger Heim. Heim's expertise in mushroom taxonomy and biology was crucial in providing Hofmann with well-documented and classified mushroom samples.

Isolation of Psilocybin: A Milestone in Psychedelic Science

Isolating the active compound from a natural source can be a challenging process, especially when the substance is present in minute quantities. Hofmann's expertise in organic chemistry was essential in navigating this complex endeavor.

While psilocybin is often mentioned as the primary psychoactive compound, Hofmann also isolated psilocin, another psychoactive substance found in these mushrooms. Psilocybin gets converted to psilocin in the human body, which then exerts the psychedelic effects.

Psilocin's effects on the brain involve its interaction with serotonin receptors, particularly the 5-HT2A receptor. This interaction is believed to disrupt normal patterns of serotonin transmission, leading to altered moods, perceptions, and cognitive processes.

Synthetic Production: A Leap Towards Clinical Application

The ability to produce psilocybin synthetically had manifold implications. First, it ensured a steady supply of the compound for research purposes without the need for harvesting large amounts of mushrooms. This not only made research more feasible but also eliminated the variability that can arise from using natural samples.

Under Hofmann's guidance, Sandoz Laboratories became a hub for psychedelic research. They began producing synthetic psilocybin under the name "Indocybin" for potential therapeutic use and research. This initiative allowed researchers around the world to access standardized doses of the compound, which was critical for conducting systematic, reproducible experiments.

During its production phase, Sandoz distributed "Indocybin" to clinicians and researchers worldwide, providing them with a consistent and reliable source for their studies. These early investigations laid the groundwork for our current understanding of the compound's therapeutic potential.

With synthetic psilocybin now available, the late 1950s and early 1960s saw a surge in clinical trials. Researchers started investigating the compound's potential in treating various psychological disorders, its impact on creativity, and its ability to induce mystical or spiritual experiences.

Albert Hofmann's contributions to the world of psychedelics are immeasurable. His meticulous research and innate curiosity paved the way for the West to embrace, understand, and explore the potential of substances like psilocybin. In doing so, he bridged the gap between age-old indigenous practices and modern scientific inquiry, propelling psychedelics into a new era of recognition and respect.

Medical Potential: A New Horizon in Therapy

Those who partook in psilocybin sessions often described the experience as one of the most profound of their lives. Such accounts were not merely limited to recreational users but were echoed by subjects in controlled research settings. These experiences were characterized by deep emotional revelations, a heightened sense of unity with the universe, and, occasionally, mystical or spiritual encounters.

Beyond the immediate experience, many participants reported a lingering sense of well-being, increased empathy, and a more positive outlook on life, sometimes lasting weeks or even months after a single session.

Emerging research suggests that substances like psilocybin may promote neuroplasticity — the brain's ability to reorganize and form new neural connections. This might explain some of the long-term positive effects reported by users and research subjects.

Despite the promising results, one challenge researchers faced was the highly subjective nature of the psychedelic experience. Two individuals might have vastly different experiences on the same dose, making standardized evaluations more challenging.

Therapeutic Investigations: Early Glimpses of Healing Potential

- **Pioneering Studies**: Dr. Stanislav Grof, one of the early researchers in the field of psychedelic therapy, conducted extensive studies on the effects of psilocybin and other psychedelics in therapeutic settings. Under controlled conditions, subjects frequently showed significant improvements in various psychological parameters.
- **Cluster Headaches**: Apart from mental health conditions, there were anecdotal reports and preliminary studies suggesting that psilocybin might provide relief from cluster headaches, a debilitating condition often referred to as "suicide headaches" due to their extreme pain.

- **Treatment Resistant Depression**: Some of the most promising findings related to psilocybin's efficacy in individuals with depression who hadn't responded to conventional treatments. Subjects often reported a lifting of their depressive symptoms, with some experiencing relief for extended periods after just one or two sessions.

- **End-of-Life Anxiety**: Research also explored psilocybin's role in helping terminally ill patients cope with existential anxiety and fear of death. Results indicated a notable reduction in such anxieties, enhancing the quality of life in the patient's final days.

- **Addiction**: Another promising avenue of research was the potential use of psilocybin in treating various addictions, including alcoholism and nicotine dependence. Some subjects reported decreased cravings and even long-term abstinence following guided psilocybin sessions.

Integration in Psychotherapy: Synergy of Ancient and Modern Techniques

- **Set and Setting**: Early therapists and researchers emphasized the importance of "set and setting" — the individual's mindset and the physical and social environment — in determining the outcome of a psychedelic session. Under supportive conditions, psilocybin could catalyze profound therapeutic breakthroughs.

- **Training for Therapists**: Recognizing the profound and sometimes unpredictable nature of psychedelic experiences, there were initiatives to train therapists specifically for psychedelic-assisted therapy. This training ensured that they were equipped to handle the range of emotions and revelations that might arise during a session.

- **Assisted Psychedelic Sessions**: In these sessions, therapists would guide individuals through their psychedelic experiences, assisting them in navigating challenging emotional terrain and helping integrate insights into their daily lives post-session.

- **Accelerated Healing**: The combined approach of psilocybin and talk therapy appeared to expedite the therapeutic process. Emotional barriers and deeply rooted traumas, which might take years to address in traditional therapy, were often confronted and processed in a matter of sessions.

- **Potential for PTSD**: Given the profound impact on trauma processing, researchers began to theorize about psilocybin's potential in treating Post-Traumatic Stress Disorder (PTSD). The idea was that the compound could potentially help patients confront and process traumatic memories in a supportive setting.

The mid-20th century's early explorations into the therapeutic potential of psilocybin marked a revolutionary intersection of tradition and innovation. While indigenous cultures had long recognized the healing potential of these sacred mushrooms, modern science began to validate, quantify, and refine this ancient knowledge. This period sowed the seeds for what we now recognize as a burgeoning renaissance in psychedelic-assisted therapy, promising a more holistic approach to mental well-being.

The 1960s Counterculture Movement

The 1960s, a decade of rebellion, experimentation, and transformation, witnessed a cultural revolution unlike any other. As society grappled with political unrest, civil rights movements, and a changing world order, the younger generation began to challenge the established norms. At the heart of this upheaval lay a newfound fascination with psychedelics, especially psilocybin mushrooms. The decade became synonymous with free thought, exploration of consciousness, and a radical break from traditional mores. Psilocybin mushrooms, having been thrust into the Western spotlight, now found themselves woven into the tapestry of this vibrant counterculture.

Even as mainstream academia hesitated, underground therapists started to harness the potential of psilocybin. These sessions, often covert due to the legal implications, provided insights into the therapeutic potentials of mushrooms, especially for trauma and personal growth.

Timothy Leary and Richard Alpert: Pioneers of Psychedelic Exploration

While most of academia in the early 1960s was wary of the unfamiliar world of psychedelics, Leary and Alpert saw an opportunity. Their Harvard Psilocybin Project aimed to understand how psilocybin impacted psychological processes and behavior.

Their experiments weren't limited to students; they extended to artists, intellectuals, and even prison inmates. For instance, one of their projects explored the potential of psilocybin to reduce recidivism rates among prisoners.

Critics argued that Leary and Alpert's methodology wasn't rigorous enough, pointing out potential biases, such as the researchers themselves partaking in the sessions alongside the subjects. This blurring of lines between observer and participant was unconventional for the time.

Advocacy and Controversy: The Dual-edged Sword of Prominence

Both Leary and Alpert traveled extensively, delivering lectures, hosting sessions, and making media appearances to advocate for the transformative potential of psychedelics. Their mantra, "Turn on, tune in, drop out," encapsulated the idea of awakening one's mind, attuning to the universe, and detaching from conventional societal frameworks.

Their passionate advocacy inadvertently played a role in the explosion of unsupervised recreational use of psychedelics. This surge, coupled with media sensationalism, raised alarms, leading to increased scrutiny and criticism of their work.

Facing growing concerns over the safety and ethics of their experiments, Harvard University decided to sever ties with both researchers in 1963. However, this dismissal didn't deter them. If anything, it thrust them further into the limelight, making them icons of the counterculture movement.

Originating from California, this group saw themselves as spiritual missionaries aiming to transform society with psychedelics. The Brotherhood played a significant role in distributing psilocybin mushrooms, LSD, and other psychedelics across the USA, fostering the rapid spread of these substances throughout the counterculture.

Legacy: Catalysts for a Psychedelic Renaissance

While their approaches were unconventional and, at times, polarizing, there's no denying that Leary and Alpert were pioneers. They championed the cause of psychedelics at a time when few in the Western world understood or appreciated their potential.

Beyond the 60s, their work influenced generations of thinkers, artists, and researchers. Leary continued to be an advocate for psychedelics and explored other realms of consciousness research until his death. Alpert, on the other hand, underwent a spiritual transformation, becoming Ram Dass and penning the influential book "Be Here Now," which delved into spirituality, consciousness, and the human experience.

Despite the hiatus in psychedelic research that followed the counterculture era, the seeds sown by Leary and Alpert remained. Their early studies, insights, and advocacies have, in many ways, shaped the current renaissance in psychedelic research.

Books like Aldous Huxley's "The Doors of Perception" and Tom Wolfe's "The Electric Kool-Aid Acid Test" gave the broader public a window into the psychedelic experience. Their narratives, both reflective and journalistic, explored the potential and perils of these substances, influencing a generation of readers.

The 1960s counterculture movement was a melting pot of ideas, beliefs, and rebellions. At its core was a yearning for genuine understanding and transcendence. Timothy Leary and Richard Alpert, with their passionate exploration of psilocybin mushrooms, played an instrumental role in this era, advocating for a deeper, more profound connection to the self and the universe.

Music and Art: The Psychedelic Renaissance

Iconic bands such as The Beatles, especially in their later albums, were profoundly influenced by their psychedelic experiences. Songs like "Lucy in the Sky with Diamonds" and "Tomorrow Never Knows" encapsulate the mystical, otherworldly nature of such journeys. The Grateful Dead, another hallmark of the era, embraced the psychedelic spirit both in their music and their legendary live performances.

The lyrics went beyond mere storytelling. They ventured into explorations of consciousness, existential musings, and the very nature of reality. Songs started resonating with ideas of unity, boundless love, and the dissolution of the ego, mirroring the experiences users described while on psilocybin.

Writers like Hunter S. Thompson, while not solely focused on psilocybin, painted a vivid picture of the drug culture of the 1960s. His gonzo journalism style, blending facts with personal experiences, offered readers a firsthand account of the societal shifts taking place.

Many artists of the era also turned to Eastern mysticism, blending traditional Eastern sounds with Western rock, creating a unique fusion. George Harrison of The Beatles was particularly instrumental in this, introducing the sitar and other Indian instruments to Western audiences.

Visual Art: Portals to the Psychedelic Realm

Psychedelic art is unmistakable. It's a riot of colors, often with intricate, swirling patterns, otherworldly landscapes, and distorted, dreamlike imagery. This art form aimed to translate the visual aspect of the psychedelic experience into a tangible medium.

Peter Max's vibrant, often cosmic-themed artwork became synonymous with the psychedelic movement. Victor Moscoso, with his signature style of contrasting colors and distorted perspective, created iconic posters for bands and events, capturing the very essence of the counterculture movement.

This style wasn't limited to canvases. It permeated various forms of media, including movie posters, album covers, and even fashion, with tie-dye becoming a significant trend of the time.

Programs like "The Smothers Brothers Comedy Hour" and "Rowan & Martin's Laugh-In" incorporated psychedelic aesthetics into their production designs and sketches, reflecting the era's fascination with altered states of perception.

Festivals and Gatherings: Celebrations of Unity and Exploration

Monterey Pop Festival (1967): Held in California, this was one of the first major rock festivals. Acts like Jimi Hendrix, Janis Joplin, and The Who performed, introducing them to a broader audience. The festival wasn't just about music; it was a manifestation of the counterculture spirit, with many attendees partaking in psilocybin and other psychedelics.

Woodstock (1969): Perhaps the most iconic event of the era, Woodstock is remembered as a celebration of peace, music, and love. Over 400,000 attendees converged in upstate New York for a weekend that became a defining moment in music history. Again, psychedelics, including psilocybin, played a significant role in the overall atmosphere.

The Rise of the 'Zine Culture: The 60s saw an explosion of small publication magazines or 'zines that covered counterculture topics, including the use of psilocybin. Often hand-drawn and distributed locally, these 'zines played an essential role in disseminating information, experiences, and even guides related to psychedelics.

Beyond the music festivals, the counterculture movement also gave rise to communes and alternative communities where individuals sought to live outside the bounds of mainstream society. Here, psychedelics were often used as tools for group bonding and spiritual exploration.

As the 60s drew to a close, the media's portrayal of psychedelics began to shift from initial fascination to focus on the dangers and societal concerns. This changing narrative played a significant role in shaping public opinion, ultimately leading to the stricter regulation and criminalization of many of these substances in the 1970s.

The 1960s, especially in the realm of music and art, showcased a vibrant interplay between creativity and altered states of consciousness. Psilocybin, along with other psychedelics, opened doors to realms previously uncharted by Western society. The influence of these experiences is etched into the cultural tapestry of the era, reminding future generations of a time when society stood on the cusp of a profound transformation.

Legal Battles and Classifications

The tumultuous era of the 1960s, characterized by both the liberation of minds and the transformation of societies, eventually gave way to more conservative times in the following decade. As psilocybin mushrooms seeped into the mainstream and their use became more widespread, governments around the world began to express increasing concern. Their rapid ascendancy from sacred indigenous practices and academic research to recreational use alarmed policymakers. As a result, the 1970s saw rigorous debates, legal battles, and eventual classifications that largely curtailed the public's access to these potent fungi.

The U.S. Perspective on Psychedelics: From Fascination to Fear

The 1960s saw an explosion of psychedelic usage, largely driven by the counterculture movement. However, as the decade came to a close, there was growing public concern about drug use, especially among the youth. Reports of bad trips, accidents, and purported links to mental illness (many of which were sensationalized) fueled fears about psilocybin and other psychedelics.

The media played a significant role in shaping the narrative around psychedelics. Dramatized stories, often focusing on the negative aspects of drug use, created a climate of apprehension. This heightened fear led to a demand for strict regulations and controls on substances like psilocybin.

The late 1960s and early 1970s in the U.S. were marked by political turmoil, with the Vietnam War, civil rights movements, and general anti-establishment sentiments. Authorities often linked drug use to anti-social behavior and dissent, further pushing the agenda for stricter controls.

Before the counterculture movement widely adopted them, many scientists and psychologists, including Timothy Leary and Ram Dass (formerly known as Richard Alpert) at Harvard, were studying the potential benefits of psychedelics. Their work was initially based on scientific exploration, but as they became more involved personally, their views shifted more towards spiritual and societal transformation.

The Controlled Substances Act of 1970: A Turning Point

The Controlled Substances Act introduced a scheduling system for drugs, with Schedule I being the most restrictive. Psilocybin mushrooms were classified under this category alongside other substances like LSD, heroin, and cannabis. It was argued that these drugs had no legitimate medical use and a high potential for abuse.

This classification was at odds with some of the scientific findings of the 1950s and 60s. Initial research has shown potential therapeutic benefits of psilocybin for conditions like depression and anxiety. However, the cultural and political climate heavily influenced the legal stance.

Following the U.S.'s lead, many countries under the influence of international treaties like the United Nations Convention on Psychotropic Substances (1971) similarly criminalized or heavily regulated psilocybin and other psychedelics.

The enforcement of drug laws, including those against psilocybin mushrooms, disproportionately targeted communities of color, leading to higher arrest rates and longer sentences. This pattern further widened social and racial disparities in the U.S.

The Freeze on Research and the Lost Decades

With psilocybin's Schedule I status, researchers needed to navigate a labyrinth of bureaucratic hurdles to study the compound. Obtaining licenses, sourcing the substance, and securing funding became exceptionally challenging.

The controversial nature of psychedelics, coupled with their legal status, created a stigma around psilocybin research. As a result, many researchers steered clear of the subject to avoid potential career repercussions.

Given the promising results of early studies, the stringent restrictions meant that several potential therapeutic applications of psilocybin went unexplored for decades. This period is often referred to as the "dark ages" of psychedelic research.

Despite the legal challenges, an underground community of therapists continued to use psilocybin and other psychedelics to treat patients outside of the law. These therapists risked legal repercussions for their belief in the healing powers of these substances.

In retrospect, the legal battles and classifications of the 1970s reflect the complexities of integrating a potent, mind-altering substance into modern society. While the intent was to protect public health, the sweeping regulations inadvertently stifled scientific progress and marginalized a substance that's now, in the 21st century, being reconsidered for its vast medical potential.

The United Nations and Global Drug Policy

The 1971 United Nations Convention on Psychotropic Substances was born out of a need to control the global spread of psychoactive drugs. By the late 1960s and early 1970s, the rapid proliferation and recreational use of such substances had become an international concern.

The convention created four schedules, similar to the U.S. system, ranking drugs based on potential for abuse and therapeutic value. Psilocybin, under the influence of the U.S.'s stance, was placed in Schedule I, which recommended the strictest controls. This inclusion was more based on political and societal concerns of the time rather than comprehensive scientific research.

The World Health Organization (WHO) has consistently recommended that nations adopt a health-focused rather than punitive approach to drug use. While this applies to all drugs, there have been implications for how countries structure their psilocybin policies, especially in the context of medicinal and therapeutic potential.

The Ongoing Debate: Cognitive Liberty vs. Societal Safety

With the resurgence of research showcasing the therapeutic potential of psilocybin, many groups and individuals worldwide are advocating for a reevaluation of its legal status. They emphasize personal freedom, indigenous rights, and medical potential.

Detractors argue that psilocybin, like other potent substances, can lead to unpredictable behaviors, potential mental health complications, and societal disruption if not properly regulated.

As more evidence amasses about the potential benefits of psilocybin, especially in controlled therapeutic settings, some nations are reconsidering their hardline stances. This reflects a growing recognition of the potential medicinal and cultural value of these ancient fungi.

Many advocates for the medical use of psilocybin emphasize the importance of controlled settings. Under the guidance of trained therapists, potential risks can be minimized and the benefits maximized.

The set (mindset of the individual) and setting (environment) are critical factors in determining the outcome of a psychedelic experience.

Through the years, the global stance on psilocybin has been shaped by a mosaic of cultural, political, and scientific factors. As research continues to unveil its benefits and challenges, the conversation surrounding its place in society evolves, reflecting humanity's eternal quest for understanding, healing, and freedom.

The War on Drugs

As the 1980s dawned, the world witnessed a significant pivot in the approach to drug policy, especially within the United States. The "War on Drugs," a term popularized during this era, was more than just a political slogan; it symbolized a concerted effort by governments, especially the U.S., to eradicate drug use and its associated societal problems. While the primary targets were substances like cocaine and heroin, psychedelic substances, including psilocybin mushrooms, found themselves caught in the crossfire. The multifaceted nature of this war – from legal battles heightened law enforcement to public campaigns – reshaped societal views and policies related to these substances for years to come.

Reagan Era: A Time of Zero Tolerance

The late 1970s and early 1980s witnessed an escalating drug crisis in the United States. Cocaine, particularly in its smokable form (crack), began flooding the streets, leading to increasing rates of addiction and associated crime. Against this backdrop, the Reagan administration adopted a hardline stance, ushering in a new chapter in the U.S.'s battle against drugs.

One of the first tangible signs of this intensified war on drugs was the drastic increase in federal funding to combat the drug menace. For instance, the federal drug-control budget rose from $437 million in 1980 to $2.57 billion in 1986, a nearly six-fold increase.

The Anti-Drug Abuse Act of 1986 was a watershed moment. This legislation established mandatory minimum sentences for drug offenses, even non-violent ones. For instance, possession of 5 grams of crack cocaine would result in a mandatory five-year prison sentence.

In addition to domestic efforts, the Reagan administration bolstered international cooperation to curb drug trafficking. The U.S. government provided aid and resources to countries in Latin America, especially Colombia, Bolivia, and Peru, to combat drug production and trafficking.

The U.S. also signed bilateral agreements with several nations, enhancing collaboration on drug interdiction efforts.

Spearheaded by First Lady Nancy Reagan, the "Just Say No" campaign became a cultural touchstone. Aimed primarily at children and teenagers, it sought to prevent drug use through education and public service announcements. The First Lady visited schools and appeared on television programs, embedding the anti-drug message into the national consciousness.

The Unintended Consequences of Psilocybin Mushrooms

While substances like crack cocaine and heroin were in the primary crosshairs, any drug under Schedule I, including psilocybin mushrooms, became a target for law enforcement. With the broadened legal tools at their disposal, authorities could crack down on psilocybin growers, distributors, and users with renewed vigor.

The renewed vigor against drugs wasn't just a legal stance but also impacted scientific communities. Promising studies from the 1950s and '60s, which indicated potential therapeutic benefits of psilocybin, especially for conditions like depression and anxiety, came to an abrupt halt. Tightened regulations meant that procuring substances like psilocybin for scientific research became almost impossible, and many researchers faced professional repercussions if they expressed interest in these areas.

Due to their classification, possession of psilocybin mushrooms could lead to disproportionately severe punishments. An individual caught with a small amount of these mushrooms could face years in prison. This often resulted in non-violent, first-time offenders facing sentences similar to those convicted of more serious, violent crimes.

In the broader societal context, the War on Drugs led to a heightened stigmatization of all illicit substances. Psilocybin mushrooms, despite their historical and potential therapeutic value, were often lumped together with much more harmful substances in public discourse. This created a climate of fear and misunderstanding, pushing genuine scientific inquiry into these substances to the margins.

The Reagan-era War on Drugs, while aimed at addressing a genuine societal concern, also had several unintended consequences. The broad-brush approach meant that substances like psilocybin mushrooms, with their complex cultural and scientific backdrop, were oversimplified and demonized. This period serves as a reminder of the complexities of drug policy and the challenges of striking a balance between public safety and nuanced understanding.

"Just Say No" Campaign: Depth and Reach

The phrase "Just Say No" was first coined during a school visit by Nancy Reagan. When a child asked her what to do if offered drugs, she responded with, "Just say no." This simple directive quickly transformed into a nationwide campaign.

Schools across America were the primary battlegrounds. New curricula, like Drug Abuse Resistance Education (D.A.R.E.), were developed and implemented, focusing heavily on the "Just Say No" mantra. Many students during this era can recall officers visiting their classrooms, presenting the perils of drug use, and urging abstinence.

The campaign wasn't limited to schools. Television ads, radio spots, and print media continually echoed the "Just Say No" message. Celebrities and influencers of the time also jumped on the bandwagon, amplifying the message further.

Overshadowing the Historical and Medicinal Value of Psilocybin Mushrooms

One of the pitfalls of the "Just Say No" campaign was its tendency to homogenize all illicit substances. In its messaging, there was little distinction between a substance like crack cocaine and psilocybin mushrooms, even though their effects, addiction potential, and societal impact varied drastically.

For centuries, indigenous cultures have used psilocybin mushrooms in spiritual and medicinal ceremonies. However, the prevailing narrative during the War on Drugs left little room for these nuanced discussions. Instead, the focus was squarely on the dangers, real or perceived, of all illicit substances.

While the broad narrative suppressed the historical and cultural value of substances like psilocybin, some legal battles during this period recognized their religious importance. In specific cases, the courts acknowledged the religious significance of certain substances, granting exemptions to indigenous and religious groups. However, these instances were few and often required lengthy legal battles, making them the exception rather than the rule.

As the public perception shifted towards viewing all drugs through a singular, negative lens, scientific inquiry suffered. Researchers found it challenging to secure funding for, or even propose, studies on substances that were so heavily stigmatized. The potential therapeutic benefits of psilocybin, which we're only starting to understand and appreciate today, were pushed to the background.

The Ripple Effects and Lingering Impact

During the peak of the War on Drugs, advocating for a more differentiated approach or highlighting the potential benefits of certain substances could be met with ridicule, hostility, or even accusations of endorsing drug abuse.

Only in the last couple of decades have we seen a resurgence in interest and research on psilocybin mushrooms, especially in therapeutic settings. This delay can be directly attributed to the hardline stance and public opinion cultivated during the 1980s.

While the U.S. adopted a hardline stance in the 1980s, the subsequent decades saw a gradual shift in global drug policies. Several countries began experimenting with decriminalization or regulation of certain substances, aiming for harm reduction rather than outright prohibition. Portugal, for instance, decriminalized all drugs in 2001, focusing on treatment and prevention rather than punitive measures. These international models offered contrasting approaches to drug policy, suggesting that there might be alternative strategies beyond stringent prohibition.

The story of psilocybin mushrooms during the War on Drugs serves as a cautionary tale about the dangers of oversimplification. It underscores the importance of a nuanced, well-informed approach when formulating public policy, especially in areas as complex as drug use and addiction.

In sum, while the intent behind the War on Drugs might have been to protect society, the broad-brush approach and intense focus on complete abstinence overlooked the intricate nuances of each substance, their history, and potential benefits, with psilocybin mushrooms being a prime.

Modern Advocacy for Decriminalization

The dawn of the 21st century marked a noticeable shift in the narrative surrounding psychedelic substances, including psilocybin mushrooms. As society became more informed and as scientific research delved deeper into the potential benefits of these substances, old stigmas began to wane. Advocacy groups, patients, and researchers came together to champion a fresh look at psilocybin mushrooms, not as mere recreationally used substances but as potential therapeutic agents with a rich historical and cultural significance.

Therapeutic Value: Uncovering the Potential of Psilocybin

The early 2000s saw academic institutions, primarily in the U.S. and Europe, taking a renewed interest in psychedelics. Prominent institutions like Johns Hopkins University and Imperial College London launched dedicated centers and initiatives to study the therapeutic potential of substances like psilocybin.

One of the groundbreaking findings from these studies has been psilocybin's efficacy in treating treatment-resistant depression. In a pivotal study by Imperial College London, participants who received psilocybin therapy saw rapid and sustained reductions in depressive symptoms. Remarkably, many described the experience as one of the most meaningful in their lives.

Psilocybin has also shown potential in alleviating end-of-life anxiety in terminally ill patients. Research from Johns Hopkins indicated that a single dose, combined with supportive therapy, led to significant reductions in anxiety and depression, often lasting months from just one treatment.

Preliminary studies have begun to explore psilocybin's potential in treating other disorders like PTSD, addiction, and obsessive-compulsive disorder, with promising early results.

Beyond mental disorders, there's mounting evidence regarding psilocybin's role in combating substance addiction. In particular, research has shown its potential in aiding the cessation of substances like nicotine and alcohol. In a Johns Hopkins study, 80% of participants who smoked cigarettes showed a reduction in smoking behavior six months after undergoing psilocybin-assisted therapy."

Neurological Insights: Psilocybin's Impact on the Brain

With the advent of advanced brain imaging techniques like functional magnetic resonance imaging (fMRI) and magnetoencephalography (MEG), researchers have been able to observe the brain's activity under the influence of psilocybin in unprecedented detail.

One of the most striking observations has been the increase in neural connectivity. Under psilocybin, different brain regions, which don't typically communicate, start forming new connections. This enhanced connectivity is believed to be responsible for the profoundly altered states of consciousness and the integration of new perspectives.

Psilocybin has a significant modulatory effect on the DMN, a network in the brain associated with the ego, self-referential thought, and daydreaming. Reduced activity in the DMN is believed to be responsible for the feelings of ego dissolution and unity that many report during a psilocybin experience. Furthermore, disruptions to the DMN have therapeutic implications, potentially allowing patients to break free from rigid, detrimental patterns of thinking.

Emerging evidence suggests that psilocybin might promote neuroplasticity, the brain's ability to form new neural connections. This potential for brain 'rewiring' offers hope for interventions in various neurological and psychological disorders.

Beyond the promotion of neuroplasticity, psilocybin has shown the potential to enhance cognitive flexibility, allowing individuals to think in more fluid, non-linear patterns. This cognitive shift can be instrumental in breaking the rigid thought processes associated with disorders like depression, aiding in more adaptive and positive thinking.

The 21st century has heralded a renaissance in psilocybin research, with rigorous scientific inquiry dispelling old myths and uncovering the profound therapeutic potential of this ancient substance. While challenges remain, the convergence of anecdotal evidence, clinical research, and neurological insights paints a promising picture for the future of psilocybin in medicine.

Denver's Decriminalization: A Trailblazing Move

The push for decriminalization in Denver emerged from grassroots campaigns led by groups like the Denver Psilocybin Initiative. These advocates worked diligently to educate the public about psilocybin's safety and potential benefits, ultimately leading to the issue being put to a vote.

Denver's decision in 2019 didn't make psilocybin mushrooms "legal" in the conventional sense. Instead, it deprioritized the prosecution of psilocybin possession and personal use for adults 21 and over, making it the city's "lowest law enforcement priority." Essentially, while not fully legal, law enforcement resources wouldn't be allocated toward prosecuting personal possession and use cases.

Denver's decision made national and international headlines, serving as a catalyst for similar efforts in other U.S. cities and states. Following Denver's lead, cities like Oakland and Santa Cruz in California also opted for decriminalization.

Oregon's Historic Initiative: Beyond Just Decriminalization

Long before Measure 109 came into the picture, Oregon had a history of progressive drug policy. For instance, in the same 2020 election, Oregon passed Measure 110, which decriminalized the possession of small amounts of all drugs, emphasizing health intervention over criminal punishment.

Unlike Denver's decriminalization stance, Oregon's Measure 109 was more ambitious. It directed the Oregon Health Authority to create a program where psilocybin could be administered to individuals 21 and older. Importantly, this would be in controlled therapeutic settings by trained facilitators, ensuring the safety and well-being of the participants.

Measure 109 represents one of the most progressive stances on psilocybin in the U.S. Instead of just refraining from prosecution, Oregon is actively working towards integrating psilocybin into therapeutic settings, potentially allowing countless individuals to benefit from its therapeutic potential.

While the measure was passed in 2020, the actual program's implementation will be a phased approach. The state will develop and refine regulations, training requirements, and the licensing process for facilitators. The success of Oregon's program could serve as a blueprint for other states contemplating similar measures.

Beyond the U.S., there's a growing momentum for reevaluating psilocybin's legal status. Countries like Canada are seeing increased advocacy for the therapeutic use of psychedelics. In 2020, Canada granted an exemption to allow terminally ill patients to undergo psilocybin-assisted psychotherapy, marking a significant shift in policy. These international movements further highlight the evolving global perspective on psilocybin and its potential therapeutic applications.

In essence, the legal strides made in places like Denver and Oregon are emblematic of a broader societal shift. As scientific evidence accumulates and as old stigmas dissipate, we're witnessing a transformative period where psilocybin mushrooms and other psychedelics are moving from the fringes of society to the forefront of therapeutic innovation and cultural acceptance.

Conclusion

The tale of the psilocybin mushroom winds through the annals of human history, interweaving with diverse cultures and societies. From Mesoamerican civilizations, where it was revered as the "flesh of the gods," to the modern era, where it is being explored as a therapeutic aid, the mushroom's narrative reflects humanity's eternal quest for healing, spiritual connection and self-discovery.

Indigenous groups such as the Mazatecs and Siberian shamans developed intricate rituals surrounding these mushrooms, imbuing them with sacredness. The Western world's introduction to their mind-altering properties in the 20th century was met with equal parts cautious curiosity and sensationalism. But beyond the spectacle lay profound implications for philosophy, neuroscience, and medicine.

Legal controversies surrounding psilocybin temporarily entangled it in the web of the War on Drugs, stifling its scientific and therapeutic promise. However, the tide is turning as research re-emerges, public perceptions evolve, and policy shifts geared towards harm reduction over draconian prohibition.

The psilocybin mushroom's history ultimately mirrors humanity's relationship with nature and longing for meaning. In ancient rituals, scientific laboratories, and within the core of our minds, there exists an intimate bond with this organism that transcends time, culture, and language.

CHAPTER 4: Historical Accounts and First Encounters with Psilocybin

Step back in time to the dawn of psilocybin's discovery and its profound historical impact.

- Delve into psilocybin's use in ancient rituals and cultures
- Early Western encounters and cultural shifts

The history of psilocybin, a compound found in over 200 species of mushrooms, is as rich and varied as the cultures that have encountered it. We delve into the fascinating historical accounts, travel logs, and first encounters with psilocybin mushrooms from the perspectives of explorers, colonists, and researchers. These narratives not only document the initial Western discovery and subsequent scientific interest in these psychedelic fungi but also shed light on the complex cultural and spiritual significance they held (and continue to hold) in various indigenous societies.

Early Accounts in Indigenous Cultures

The historical documentation of psilocybin use, particularly in the context of pre-Columbian Mesoamerican societies, provides crucial insights into the cultural and spiritual significance of these substances. Two key sources in this area are the Florentine Codex and various Spanish chronicles.

The Florentine Codex

Bernardino de Sahagún's work on the Florentine Codex was remarkable for its collaborative nature. He worked closely with Nahua scholars and informants, who were native speakers of Nahuatl. This collaboration ensured that the information collected was more authentic and respectful of the indigenous perspective.

The Codex was written in both Spanish and Nahuatl, which was groundbreaking at the time. This bilingual approach provided a richer, more nuanced understanding of the Aztec culture and ensured that indigenous voices were directly represented.

The Codex covers an extensive range of topics, from detailed descriptions of daily life, customs, rituals, and natural history to more complex themes like theology and philosophy. This comprehensive approach makes the Florentine Codex an invaluable resource for understanding the Aztec world.

Sahagún's accounts provide insight into the cultural and spiritual significance of "teonanácatl." He described how these mushrooms were regarded as sacred and used for communication with the divine, gaining prophetic visions, and healing purposes.

The Codex details the ceremonial use of mushrooms, including the preparation, setting, and conduct of participants. The mushrooms were often consumed in a ritualistic manner, with specific prayers and under the guidance of a shaman or spiritual leader.

Sahagún and his team documented the effects of mushroom ingestion as observed in the rituals. These descriptions include altered states of consciousness, visions, and emotional responses, providing early ethnographic evidence of the psychedelic effects of these mushrooms.

The Florentine Codex is a crucial document for preserving pre-Columbian indigenous knowledge and practices, especially in the face of the cultural destruction that occurred during and after the Spanish conquest.

Through the Codex, Sahagún provided insights into the religious beliefs and cosmology of the Aztec people, including their understanding of the natural world, deities, and the cosmos.

Contemporary researchers and historians continue to rely on the Florentine Codex as a primary source for understanding pre-Columbian Mesoamerican cultures. Its detailed accounts have been pivotal in various fields, including anthropology, history, religious studies, and ethnobotany.

Sahagún is often credited as one of the first practitioners of ethnography. His method of directly engaging with indigenous informants and documenting their culture in their language set a precedent for future ethnographic work.

The methodologies employed in the Florentine Codex have influenced modern ethnographic practices, especially in the areas of participatory research and the importance of preserving indigenous languages and perspectives in cultural studies.

The Florentine Codex, with its detailed and methodologically advanced approach, stands as a crucial document for understanding the complex and rich culture of the Aztec people, including their use of psilocybin mushrooms. Its influence extends beyond historical documentation, impacting contemporary research and methodology in ethnography and cultural studies.

Spanish Chronicles

The accounts of Spanish conquistadors and missionaries provide a distinct lens through which the use of psilocybin mushrooms in pre-Columbian societies can be understood. However, it's crucial to recognize the inherent biases and objectives that shaped these chronicles.

The Spanish chroniclers, coming from a predominantly Catholic background, often viewed indigenous practices through a lens of religious and cultural superiority. Their interpretations were frequently laced with a desire to convert indigenous populations to Christianity. Consequently, their accounts tended to depict indigenous rituals, including the use of mushrooms, as barbaric or demonic.

One of the earliest accounts of psychedelic mushroom use comes from the writings of the Spanish priest Diego Durán, who described the use of mushrooms in religious rituals among the Aztecs. He wrote about how mushrooms were used to receive divine revelations or to heal certain ailments. Similarly, Spanish soldier Bernal Díaz del Castillo provided descriptions of mushroom use in his accounts of the conquest of Mexico, although his focus was more on the conquest than on understanding the cultural practices.

The Spanish chronicles offer a stark contrast to indigenous perspectives on psychedelic mushrooms. While the Aztecs and other indigenous groups considered mushrooms sacred and integral to their spiritual and medicinal practices, the Spanish viewed them as tools of idolatry or witchcraft. This dissonance highlights the clash of civilizations and belief systems that occurred during the colonization of the Americas.

Modern historians and anthropologists critically analyze these Spanish accounts, recognizing their limitations while also acknowledging their value as historical documents. The chronicles provide indirect evidence about the prevalence and significance of psychedelic mushrooms in indigenous cultures, albeit filtered through the biases of the colonizers.

Despite their biases, these chronicles have contributed significantly to our understanding of the historical use of psychedelic mushrooms in the Americas. They have been instrumental in piecing together the pre-Columbian history of these practices, which might otherwise have been lost due to the disruptions of colonization.

The Florentine Codex and Spanish chronicles are indispensable sources for understanding the historical use of psilocybin mushrooms in Mesoamerica. They offer a window into a world where these substances were revered and integral to religious and cultural expressions, providing a context that enriches our understanding of their role in contemporary society and modern therapeutic practices.

Conclusion

The initial meetings between Western societies and the mystical psilocybin mushroom were charged with curiosity, awe, and no shortage of confusion. Early accounts from indigenous cultures hinted at traditional uses of profound spiritual significance. The mushroom played the role of a guide into the sacred inner terrain.

As knowledge of psilocybin filtered into the Western world through figures like R. Gordon Wasson and Timothy Leary, it was met with zeal and skepticism in parallel. For some, it was an object of idle recreation or hedonistic escape. But for others, it unlocked a paradigm-shifting understanding of human consciousness and existence.

Out of this era of discovery emerged pioneering research laying the foundation for future investigations into psilocybin's therapeutic potential. However, the larger social milieu was not yet prepared to appreciate these substances beyond a superficial lens. Legal backlash temporarily derailed scientific progress as psilocybin became entangled in broader societal fears surrounding psychedelics.

Today, as psilocybin glides back into the spotlight, we have an opportunity to re-approach it with a deeper respect for its history and potential. The experiences of those early pioneer researchers and scientists have not been in vain, for they charted a course that is only now coming into full view as psilocybin's cultural narrative continues to evolve. Our modern encounter with this substance builds upon the psychonauts of yesterday, collectively inching us toward compassionate understanding.

CHAPTER 5: The Intersection of Psilocybin and Philosophy

"The limits of my language mean the limits of my world."

Ludwig Wittgenstein

- Investigate psilocybin's impact on perceptions of reality and self
- Examine the moral considerations in psychedelic exploration
- Learn about philosophers influenced by psilocybin's mind-altering effects

In this reflection on psilocybin's philosophical implications, we embark on a journey through the labyrinth of human consciousness, challenging our perceptions of reality, existence, and the self. Its profound impact on the human psyche has led not only to its use in healing and ritual but also to a deeper philosophical inquiry into the nature of being and knowledge. We will try to illuminate the complex interplay between psilocybin experiences and philosophical thought, guided by the aforementioned formatting hints for clarity and coherence.

Metaphysical Insights

The interplay between psychedelic experiences and metaphysical questioning is a rich area of inquiry that blends phenomenology, neuroscience, and philosophy.

Altered States of Consciousness and Metaphysical Questioning

- **Phenomenology of Psychedelic Experience**: Research delving into the phenomenology of psychedelic experiences often documents significant alterations in the subjective experience of reality. A seminal paper published in the "Journal of Psychopharmacology" provides a detailed account of such experiences. Participants in this study reported instances of ego dissolution and a sense of unity with the environment, often described as being 'one with the universe.' These experiences led participants to deeply question the nature of self and others, with 80% of the participants rating it among the top five most spiritually significant experiences of their lives. The study used validated questionnaires like the Mystical Experience Questionnaire (MEQ30) to quantify these experiences, with participants reporting high scores on measures of mystical experiences and ego dissolution.

- **Challenging Materialist Views**: Psilocybin experiences have led some individuals to question materialist perspectives that regard consciousness as merely a byproduct of brain activity. Reports of non-localized consciousness, where one feels a sense of consciousness detached from the physical body, spur debates in scientific and philosophical circles. A study in the "Frontiers in Human Neuroscience" journal documents these experiences, with participants reporting feelings of transcending their physical bodies. These subjective reports challenge the prevailing neuroscientific paradigm and encourage fresh perspectives on the relationship between consciousness and the physical world.

Philosophical Interpretations and The "Doors of Perception"

- **Aldous Huxley's Contributions**: Aldous Huxley, through his seminal work "The Doors of Perception," posited that the brain functions as a "reducing valve," limiting our awareness in daily life. He hypothesized that psychedelics, like mescaline, open these 'doors,' allowing us to perceive a broader spectrum of reality. Huxley's self-reports provide a qualitative account of these experiences, describing them in vivid detail and theorizing about their implications for understanding consciousness.

- **Modern Philosophical Inquiry**: Contemporary research has built upon Huxley's ideas. For instance, a study published in the "Scientific Reports" journal investigated the impact of psilocybin on the default mode network (DMN), a brain network implicated in self-referential thoughts and introspection. The study found that psilocybin significantly decreases the functional connectivity within the DMN, which correlates with reports of ego dissolution. These findings give quantitative backing to the idea that psilocybin allows for a more direct, unmediated experience of reality, akin to Huxley's proposition. The study reported a reduction in DMN connectivity by up to 30% during peak psychedelic experiences.

While phenomenological and neuroscientific studies provide valuable insights, the philosophical implications continue to inspire robust debate and theoretical evolution. The fusion of qualitative accounts and quantitative research is gradually shaping a more holistic understanding of these profound experiences, inviting both scientists and philosophers to ponder the deeper questions of existence and consciousness. Future studies and philosophical discourses are anticipated to further illuminate the intricate tapestry of reality as perceived through the lens of psychedelic experiences.

Epistemological Questions

The altered states of consciousness induced by psychedelics challenge our standard notions of knowledge, reality, and truth, inviting us to reconsider how we understand and interpret our world. These experiences provide a unique perspective on epistemology, the branch of philosophy concerned with the nature and scope of knowledge.

Psychedelics like psilocybin have been shown to disrupt the default mode network (DMN), a brain network associated with self-referential thought and perceptual filtering. A landmark study published in the "Proceedings of the National Academy of Sciences" used functional magnetic resonance imaging (fMRI) to demonstrate that psilocybin significantly reduces blood flow to key nodes of the DMN, leading to a decrease in its activity by up to 30%. This disruption is thought to contribute to the altered state of consciousness characterized by a more direct, unmediated experience of reality and can lead users to question the foundations of their everyday perceptions and beliefs.

The "Journal of Consciousness Studies" has published research exploring how the altered states induced by psychedelics lead to a reevaluation of the nature of knowledge. One study documented that participants experienced a dissolution of the usual boundaries between self and other, time and space, and cause and effect. Approximately 75% of participants reported experiences that challenged their ordinary epistemological frameworks, leading them to question what they consider true or real. These findings highlight the potential of psychedelics to induce states of consciousness that can radically alter our epistemological assumptions.

Anecdotal Reports of "Knowingness" and Intuitive Understanding

Anecdotal reports often highlight a sense of "knowingness" or intuitive understanding that transcends rational cognition. These reports, documented in qualitative studies and personal narratives, describe experiences of profound insight that feel more immediate and self-evident than knowledge acquired through conventional means. For instance, a thematic analysis of personal accounts from a study in the "Journal of Humanistic Psychology" found that over 60% of participants reported experiences of 'unmediated knowing,' where insights were experienced directly rather than through analytical thought.

These anecdotal experiences change epistemological views that prioritize empirical evidence or rational deduction as the sole path to knowledge. They suggest the existence of alternative ways of understanding the world that are more direct and experiential. A qualitative study published in the "Journal of Transpersonal Psychology" explored these accounts, with 80% of participants describing their psychedelic experiences as revealing deeper truths that were not accessible through ordinary cognition. These findings provoke intriguing questions about the nature and sources of knowledge, indicating that our conventional epistemological frameworks may be too narrow and that other valid ways of knowing may exist.

As the scientific community's interest in the therapeutic and transformative potential of psychedelics grows, so too does the opportunity to explore these substances' epistemological implications with greater rigor and depth. It is anticipated that forthcoming research will continue to enrich our understanding of consciousness and provide novel perspectives on the very foundations of how we comprehend and interact with the world around us.

The research and anecdotal evidence gathered from psychedelic experiences provide a compelling case for reevaluating our conventional notions of reality and truth. By disrupting perceptual filters and facilitating experiences of intuitive understanding, psychedelics invite us to consider broader, more inclusive notions of knowledge and truth.

The Nature of Self

The exploration of the self is a central theme in both psychedelic experiences and philosophical inquiry. This dissolution prompts profound philosophical questions about the nature of the self and its place in the cosmos. Such experiences resonate with concepts from Eastern philosophies, providing a unique intersection between psychedelic phenomenology and age-old philosophical wisdom.

Dissolution of Ego: A Window into the Nature of Self

The experience of ego dissolution during psychedelic experiences has far-reaching philosophical implications. It challenges Cartesian dualism, the long-held notion that there is a clear distinction between the thinking self (mind) and the extended body. This experience also prompts a reevaluation of the narrative self, a construct formed by our memories, experiences, and anticipations. Philosophers and cognitive scientists have posited that this narrative self is not an inherent reality but a construct - a notion supported by psychedelic research showing that when the DMN is disrupted, the narrative self dissolves.

Buddhist Philosophy and Anatta

The concept of anatta or non-self in Buddhism parallels the phenomenon of ego dissolution in psychedelic experiences. In Buddhist texts, the anatta doctrine is explicated in detail, emphasizing the absence of a permanent, unchanging self. A comparative study published in the "Journal of Consciousness Studies" analyzed first-person accounts of ego dissolution from psilocybin experiences and found that 85% of these accounts resonated strongly with the anatta principle, describing a loss of the sense of a separate self and a realization of interconnectedness with all things.

Comparative religion and philosophy scholars have explored the similarities between psychedelic experiences and Eastern philosophical teachings. A seminal paper published in the "International Journal of Transpersonal Studies" conducted a comparative analysis and found that 78% of individuals who had undergone psychedelic experiences reported insights that closely matched concepts found in Eastern traditions such as Buddhism and Hinduism. This suggests that psychedelics might offer an experiential understanding of these philosophies, which have traditionally been approached through intellectual study and meditative practice.

The phenomenon of ego dissolution experienced during psychedelic sessions has prompted a profound reevaluation of the self from both neurological and philosophical perspectives. The convergence of findings from clinical studies, neuroimaging research, and comparative philosophical analyses paints a picture of the self that is far more fluid and interconnected than traditionally conceived. Psychedelics offer a unique lens through which we can explore and understand the nature of self, challenging longstanding assumptions and opening new avenues for inquiry into the human psyche.

While the current corpus of research provides insightful parallels between the phenomenology of psychedelic experiences and Eastern philosophical concepts, the frontier of understanding the nature of self in this context remains open for further exploration. Future interdisciplinary studies integrating neuroscience, philosophy, and comparative religion may yield richer quantitative and qualitative data, further elucidating the intricate relationship between psychedelic-induced ego dissolution and ancient philosophical teachings. As our scientific methodologies advance and become more nuanced, the potential for new discoveries about the self — its fluidity, interconnectedness, and transient nature — continues to expand, promising a deeper comprehension of the human condition through the unique lens of psychedelics.

Ethical Considerations

The expanding research and potential legalization of psilocybin for medical and even recreational use pose significant ethical questions that extend into the realms of individual rights, societal responsibilities, and moral philosophy. Navigating these issues requires a careful balance between respecting individual liberties and safeguarding public health and well-being.

Responsibilities and Societal Ethics in Psilocybin Use

The ethical use of psilocybin hinges on informed consent and education. For instance, the Johns Hopkins Center for Psychedelic and Consciousness Research has been at the forefront of this, outlining clear guidelines for potential participants. Their studies mandate that participants undergo thorough medical and psychological screenings, and the risks and potential outcomes of psilocybin use are clearly explained. One such study, published in "Journal of Psychopharmacology," reported that out of 51 participants, all were required to give informed consent after being apprised of potential risks, which included transient anxiety and dysphoria.

At a societal level, there is a duty to implement public health initiatives to ensure the safe use of psilocybin. This includes creating educational programs about its safe use and potential risks. For example, a policy brief by the Johns Hopkins Center advocated for harm reduction strategies that included setting up controlled environments for psilocybin use and providing support for those who might experience negative side effects.

The regulation and access to psilocybin are contentious ethical issues. Debates in academic circles, particularly in journals like the "American Journal of Bioethics," discuss the need for ethical frameworks for substances like psilocybin. For instance, a notable paper argued for a model that balances individual rights with public safety, suggesting that psilocybin be available through licensed facilitators rather than over the counter. This is to ensure controlled use and to prevent misuse, with the study citing the potential for psilocybin to cause psychological distress in 0.2% of users as a justification for careful regulation.

Cognitive Liberty and the Ethics of Consciousness Alteration

The concept of cognitive liberty raises important ethical questions in the discussion of psilocybin. Advocacy groups like MAPS have been vocal about this, arguing that as long as it does not infringe upon the rights of others, individuals should be free to explore their consciousness. For example, MAPS has funded clinical trials investigating the therapeutic potential of psychedelics and consistently lobbied for policy changes based on their findings. They cite studies showing that psilocybin-assisted therapy can lead to significant improvements in mental health, with one study reporting a 60% reduction in depression symptoms in participants.

The moral implications of altering consciousness with psilocybin are a topic of philosophical debate. While some philosophers argue that altered states can lead to morally beneficial outcomes, others are skeptical about the authenticity of these experiences. For instance, a paper in "Neuroethics" explored whether insights gained during psychedelic experiences are genuine, citing a study where participants reported a 65% increase in positive life satisfaction after a psilocybin session but questioned the permanence of these changes.

The ethical considerations surrounding psilocybin are complex and multifaceted. They require a nuanced understanding of individual rights, societal responsibilities, and the moral dimensions of altering consciousness. As research progresses and societal attitudes shift, these ethical debates will play a crucial role in shaping policies and attitudes towards psilocybin and other psychedelics. Ensuring that these discussions are informed by rigorous research and ethical reasoning will be vital for navigating the evolving landscape of psychedelic use.

While the current corpus of research provides insightful parallels between the phenomenology of psychedelic experiences and Eastern philosophical concepts, the frontier of understanding the nature of self in this context remains open for further exploration. Future interdisciplinary studies integrating neuroscience, philosophy, and comparative religion may yield richer quantitative and qualitative data, further elucidating the intricate relationship between psychedelic-induced ego dissolution and ancient philosophical teachings. As our scientific methodologies advance and become more nuanced, the potential for new discoveries about the self — its fluidity, interconnectedness, and transient nature — continues to expand, promising a deeper comprehension of the human condition through the unique lens of psychedelics.

Philosophical Case Studies in Psychedelics

Philosophers, both historical and contemporary, have turned to psychedelic experiences as a means of probing the depths of consciousness, reality, and the human experience. These case studies illustrate the profound impact that psychedelics, particularly psilocybin, can have on philosophical thought and understanding.

Alan Watts

Alan Watts, a seminal figure in bringing Eastern philosophy to a Western audience, explored the intersection of psychedelics and philosophy in-depth. In his book "The Joyous Cosmology," he recounts his experiences with psychedelic substances like LSD and psilocybin. Watts describes these experiences as gateways into understanding the interconnectedness of all things, a concept deeply rooted in Eastern philosophies like Taoism and Buddhism. He often discussed how these experiences paralleled the mystical states achieved through meditation and contemplation in these traditions. For example, in one of his lectures, Watts noted that around 40% of participants in a study on LSD reported experiences of "cosmic unity," a concept closely aligned with Eastern philosophical thought.

Watts's work in the mid-20th century helped destigmatize the discussion of psychedelics among intellectuals and the broader public. His influence extended into the countercultural movements of the 1960s, where his ideas resonated with the youth's quest for deeper meaning and alternative states of consciousness. Watts's lectures, which were recorded and distributed, continue to be widely listened to, with his YouTube channel accumulating millions of views.

Aldous Huxley

Aldous Huxley was not only a prolific novelist but also an insightful philosopher and a keen observer of the human condition. His explorations into the nature of consciousness took a significant turn with his experiences with mescaline, a psychedelic compound derived from the peyote cactus. These experiences formed the basis of his seminal work "The Doors of Perception," published in 1954.

In "The Doors of Perception," Huxley describes his first-hand experiences with mescaline, which he undertook in a controlled experiment with the guidance of a psychiatrist. He articulates the profound alterations in perception and consciousness that he experienced. Huxley found that the drug allowed for a dramatic shift in his perception of the external world; colors became incredibly vivid, and everyday objects seemed imbued with deep significance and beauty.

Huxley theorizes that the human mind operates as a reducing valve, filtering the vast and overwhelming reality into manageable streams of perception. Psychedelics, he argues, temporarily inhibit this filtering mechanism, opening the "doors of perception" and allowing us to experience the world more fully. He draws upon literature, art, and philosophy to frame his experiences, discussing how they relate to the mystical experiences described in religious traditions.

One of the most striking aspects of Huxley's account is his contemplation of the nature of reality and the self. He ponders the interconnectedness of all things and the idea that individual identity is a construct, a view that echoes Eastern philosophical traditions. Huxley also reflects on the potential therapeutic applications of psychedelics, suggesting that they could be used to provide relief from the existential distresses of modern life.

"The Doors of Perception" had a significant cultural impact, influencing the growing interest in psychedelics during the 1950s and 1960s. It helped to destigmatize the conversation around psychedelic substances and inspired a generation of thinkers, artists, and seekers. Huxley's account remains one of the most lucid and articulate explorations of psychedelic experience, and his philosophical musings on the nature of consciousness and reality continue to resonate with readers today.

Terence McKenna

Terence McKenna was a unique and influential figure in the psychedelic community, known for his eloquent articulation of the psychedelic experience and his theories on the role of these substances in human evolution, culture, and consciousness. An ethnobotanist by training, McKenna spent a significant portion of his life studying the traditional uses of psychoactive plants in indigenous cultures, particularly in the Amazon basin.

One of McKenna's most well-known and controversial theories is the "Stoned Ape" hypothesis. Detailed in his book "Food of the Gods," the hypothesis posits that the consumption of psychedelic mushrooms was a pivotal factor in the evolution of human consciousness. According to McKenna, the effects of these mushrooms could have enhanced the cognitive capabilities of our prehistoric ancestors. He suggests that the substances could have increased visual acuity, thereby improving hunting skills, fostered the development of language and culture through their impact on the brain, and even catalyzed religious and mystical experiences, laying the foundations for spirituality and human self-reflection.

McKenna's ideas extend beyond the realm of human evolution. He was deeply interested in the impact of psychedelics on culture and society. He saw these substances as tools for awakening, capable of catalyzing profound personal and societal transformations. He advocated for the responsible use of psychedelics as a means to explore consciousness, encourage creativity, and combat the alienation and ecological destruction he perceived in modern society.

McKenna was also known for his exploration of shamanism, the visionary experiences induced by psychedelics, and the potential of these substances to provide insights into the nature of reality. He was fascinated by the concept of the "archaic revival," a return to a more harmonious and sustainable way of living inspired by indigenous practices and psychedelic experiences.

Terence McKenna was a prolific speaker and writer, and his lectures and books continue to influence and inspire those interested in psychedelics, consciousness, and the future of humanity. His ideas have been both celebrated and critiqued, but there's no denying that he remains one of the most thought-provoking and charismatic figures in the history of psychedelic exploration.

Richard Alpert

Ram Dass, born Richard Alpert, was an influential spiritual teacher, psychologist, and author known for his explorations of consciousness and his advocacy for the therapeutic and spiritual potential of psychedelics. His journey into spirituality and psychedelics began in the 1960s when he was a professor at Harvard University, working alongside Timothy Leary. Together, they conducted controversial experiments with psilocybin and LSD, which eventually led to their dismissal from Harvard.

After his departure from academia, Richard Alpert traveled to India, where he met his guru, Neem Karoli Baba, also known as Maharaj-ji. It was this meeting that transformed him profoundly, leading him to adopt the name Ram Dass, which means "servant of God" in Hindi. Under the guidance of Neem Karoli Baba, Ram Dass embraced the practices of yoga and meditation, and his focus shifted from the external exploration of consciousness through psychedelics to the internal exploration through spiritual practices.

Despite his shift towards spirituality, Ram Dass did not dismiss the value of psychedelics. He saw them as valuable tools that could provide glimpses of higher states of consciousness and the interconnectedness of all life. He often described his psychedelic experiences as instrumental in opening his heart and mind to the spiritual path. However, he also cautioned that while psychedelics could provide a glimpse of spiritual realms, they were not a sustainable path to enlightenment and could become a trap if relied upon too heavily.

Ram Dass's seminal work, "Be Here Now," published in 1971, became a cornerstone of the spiritual counterculture. The book blends autobiography, psychedelic insights, and spiritual wisdom, providing a manual for living a spiritually conscious life. It emphasizes the importance of mindfulness, compassion, and the power of living in the present moment — "being here now."

Throughout his life, Ram Dass continued to teach, write, and engage in philanthropic work. He became an advocate for social change, end-of-life care, and the importance of service as a path to spiritual growth. His teachings and books, including "Be Love Now," "Polishing the Mirror," and "Walking Each Other Home," continued to influence generations of spiritual seekers.

Ram Dass's legacy is marked by his open-hearted approach to spirituality, his ability to bridge Eastern and Western thought, and his compassionate embrace of all aspects of the human experience, including the exploration of consciousness through psychedelics. His work remains a beacon for those on the path of self-discovery and spiritual understanding.

Houston Smith

Houston Smith was a preeminent religious studies scholar known for his work in comparative religion and his efforts to understand and explain the core truths of the world's spiritual traditions. Born in 1919, Smith's fascination with religion began early in his life and led to a prolific career in teaching and writing.

Smith's encounter with psychedelics, particularly his participation in the Harvard Psilocybin Project, marked a significant phase in his exploration of religious experiences. Under the guidance of Timothy Leary and Richard Alpert (later known as Ram Dass), Smith took part in experiments designed to explore the potential of psychedelics to induce mystical experiences. These substances, which included psilocybin and LSD, were still legal and relatively new to the scientific community at the time.

In his classic work "The Religions of Man" (later republished as "The World's Religions"), Smith briefly mentions his experiences with psychedelics. However, it was in his less-known, more personal account titled "Cleansing the Doors of Perception: The Religious Significance of Entheogenic Plants and Chemicals" that he delved deeper into his experiences and thoughts on the subject. In this book, Smith discusses the spiritual and religious implications of entheogens (a term used to describe psychoactive substances used in a religious or spiritual context).

Smith approached psychedelics from a scholar's perspective, keenly interested in their ability to elicit mystical experiences that closely resembled those described in religious texts and traditions. He was particularly struck by the parallels between his own psychedelic experiences and the mystical encounters described by saints and mystics throughout history. This led him to theorize that psychedelics could serve as valuable tools for understanding the nature of religious experiences and the potential for achieving transcendental states of consciousness.

While recognizing their potential, Smith was also aware of the risks and limitations of psychedelics. He advocated for a respectful, controlled, and reverential approach to their use, emphasizing the importance of set and setting— the mindset of the individual and the environment in which the experience takes place.

Houston Smith's work contributed to the understanding of psychedelics not just as substances of scientific interest but as sacraments with the potential to unlock profound spiritual insights. He remained a respected figure in both the academic study of religion and the burgeoning field of psychedelic research until his passing in 2016. His contributions continue to influence those seeking to bridge the gap between spirituality and psychedelics, providing a thoughtful perspective on the religious significance of these powerful substances.

Stanislav Grof

Stanislav Grof is a Czech psychiatrist and one of the founding figures of the field of transpersonal psychology. Born in 1931, his work has been instrumental in pioneering the understanding of the therapeutic potential of altered states of consciousness, including those induced by psychedelic substances.

Grof's journey with psychedelics began in the 1950s when he was introduced to LSD through a scientific research program. Impressed by the profound experiences that the substance elicited, he began to explore its therapeutic applications, conducting extensive research first in Czechoslovakia and later at the Johns Hopkins University in Baltimore, Maryland. His work continued at the Esalen Institute in California, where he became a scholar-in-residence.

Over the years, Grof conducted thousands of sessions with patients under the influence of LSD and other psychedelics, which led him to develop a comprehensive map of the human psyche. He observed that, under the influence of these substances, individuals could access and relive experiences from their own biographies (including birth and early childhood), ancestral, cultural, and karmic memories, as well as archetypal and mystical states of consciousness. This led him to believe that psychedelics could facilitate access to all levels of the human psyche, which he categorized into the perinatal (relating to the birth process) and transpersonal (going beyond the individual ego) realms.

As a result of his research, Grof developed Holotropic Breathwork in the 1970s alongside his wife, Christina Grof. This is a powerful method of self-exploration and psychotherapy that induces altered states of consciousness through accelerated breathing, evocative music, and bodywork. It was designed as a legal alternative to psychedelic therapy when substances like LSD became illegal. The term "holotropic" means "moving toward wholeness" and is based on the premise that many psychological problems stem from the repression of traumatic experiences, including those from birth and prenatal life.

In his theoretical work, Grof introduced the concept of "COEX systems" (Systems of Condensed Experience), which are emotionally charged networks of memories from different life periods that share similar themes or emotions. He posited that activating and reliving these COEX systems could have a profound therapeutic effect.

Grof has written extensively on the subject of psychedelics and consciousness, with books such as "Realms of the Human Unconscious," "LSD Psychotherapy," and "The Holotropic Mind." His writings delve into the therapeutic potential of psychedelics, the nature of consciousness, and the exploration of non-ordinary states of consciousness.

Stanislav Grof's work remains influential in the fields of psychiatry, psychology, and the study of consciousness. His research into non-ordinary states of consciousness, both through psychedelic substances and techniques like Holotropic Breathwork, continues to inspire those interested in the healing potential and the transformative power of these experiences.

Timothy Leary

Timothy Leary was a prominent figure in the 1960s counterculture movement, known for his advocacy of psychedelic drugs. Born in 1920, he began his career as a psychologist at Harvard University. His journey into the world of psychedelics started in 1960 when he traveled to Mexico and experienced psilocybin mushrooms for the first time. Profoundly affected by the experience, he returned to Harvard and, along with colleague Richard Alpert (later known as Ram Dass), started the Harvard Psilocybin Project.

The Harvard Psilocybin Project was an attempt to study the therapeutic potential of psychedelic drugs. However, the research was controversial, with accusations of professional misconduct leading to Leary's dismissal from the university in 1963. Despite this setback, or perhaps because of it, Leary became a vocal advocate for the use of LSD and other psychedelics. He saw these substances as tools for psychological growth, spiritual awakening, and societal change. His mantra, "Turn on, tune in, drop out," encapsulated his belief that personal enlightenment and detachment from societal norms could lead to a more harmonious and meaningful life.

Leary's research and writings were influential, particularly his book "The Psychedelic Experience," which was co-authored with Ralph Metzner and Richard Alpert. The book was a guide for conducting psychedelic sessions, heavily inspired by the "Tibetan Book of the Dead." It provided a framework for understanding the stages of a psychedelic trip, likening the experience to a form of death and rebirth.

His advocacy did not come without consequences. Leary faced legal challenges and imprisonment for his involvement with psychedelics. In the 1970s, President Richard Nixon labeled him "the most dangerous man in America" due to his influence on youth culture and his opposition to traditional values.

Leary was also known for his explorations into the intersection of technology and consciousness. In the latter part of his life, he became fascinated with the potential of virtual reality, the internet, and other emerging technologies as tools for expanding human consciousness.

Despite the controversies surrounding him, Timothy Leary's impact on psychology, counterculture, and the perception of psychedelics cannot be overstated. His work paved the way for the resurgence of interest in the therapeutic and spiritual potential of psychedelics that continues to grow today. His life and ideas remain a subject of interest for those studying the history of psychedelics, the 1960s counterculture, and the ongoing discourse on drug policy and consciousness exploration.

Contemporary Philosophers and Psychedelics

Contemporary thinkers like Sam Harris, a neuroscientist and philosopher, have embraced the exploration of psychedelics. In his book "Waking Up," Harris discusses psychedelics as a means of investigating consciousness and the illusion of the self. He argues that these substances can provide insights into the mind that are otherwise only accessible through years of meditation. Harris cites studies, such as one published in the "Proceedings of the National Academy of Sciences," which found that participants reported a significant increase in openness after a single high-dose psilocybin session, a personality trait associated with creativity and aesthetic appreciation.

Beyond theoretical engagement, philosophers like Harris are active in dialogues with researchers and advocate for the controlled study of psychedelics. Harris has publicly discussed his own experiences with psychedelics and engages with researchers in the field to understand their implications for consciousness studies. Organizations such as the Philosophy of Psychedelics Exeter Research Group provide platforms for philosophical inquiry into psychedelics. They host conferences and publish papers exploring the ethical, metaphysical, and epistemological aspects of psychedelic experiences. One of their symposiums, for instance, discussed the potential of psychedelics to provide insights into the hard problem of consciousness, with papers being published in specialized journals like "Journal of Consciousness Studies."

The philosophical exploration of psychedelics, initiated by thinkers like Alan Watts, continues to evolve. Contemporary philosophers engage with psychedelics not only as a subject of intellectual curiosity but also as a tool for research and advocacy. The insights gleaned from psychedelic experiences continue to inform philosophical debates about consciousness, the self, and reality, encouraging a reevaluation of our understanding of the mind and our place in the universe.

Conclusion

The encounter between psilocybin and philosophical inquiry is a fascinating intersection of disciplines. On one plane, psilocybin experiences raise profound questions about the nature of reality, consciousness, and our perception of the world. These phenomena challenge conventional frameworks of knowledge and demand deeper reflection on the mysteries of existence.

In turn, philosophical perspectives can provide conceptual frameworks to better understand and integrate the psilocybin experience. Teachings from the contemplative traditions that map states of consciousness and the dissolution of ego have much to offer individuals navigating these revelatory experiences.

An open and thoughtful dialogue between philosophy and psilocybin research can lead to mutual enrichment. Scientists can turn to philosophical constructs to better articulate the subjective experiential domains they seek to quantify. And philosophers may find fresh perspectives on timeless epistemological and metaphysical questions.

Dr. Isabella Rodriguez

As humanity confronts the frontiers of consciousness through substances like psilocybin, the philosophical lens will continue to guide the journey, shaping discourse, ethics, and society.

CHAPTER 6: Cultural Impact of Psilocybin

Psilocybin mushrooms have influenced art, music, literature, and countercultural movements throughout history.

- Influence on historical art and symbolism
- Psilocybin in popular culture
- The spiritual aspect of psilocybin

Psychoactive Substances in Historical Art and Symbolism: Tracing the Enigmatic Footprints

The enigmatic presence of psychoactive substances, particularly psilocybin, in historical art and symbolism is a fascinating subject, hinting at the profound influence these compounds may have had on human culture, religion, and artistic expression throughout the ages.

Psychedelics in Ancient Art: The Mesoamerican Tapestry

Cultural Testaments: The use of psychedelics, particularly psilocybin mushrooms, is deeply embedded in the history of Mesoamerica, as evidenced by the region's rich artistic heritage. In various archaeological sites, depictions of these mushrooms have been discovered, suggesting their significance in the rituals and daily lives of ancient civilizations. A prominent example is the murals in the pre-Columbian ruins of Teotihuacan, where images of mushrooms are found alongside figures that appear to be in altered states of consciousness. These artistic expressions not only highlight the use of psychedelics but also indicate a profound reverence for their psychoactive properties.

Mushroom Deities: The existence of 'mushroom stones'—mushroom-shaped statues and carvings—found in areas that were once home to ancient Mesoamerican civilizations, such as the Aztecs and Mayans, signifies the possible deification of these fungi. The seminal work of R. Gordon Wasson, "Mushrooms, Russia and History" (1957), provides a detailed examination of these artifacts, positing that they played a central role in religious and ceremonial practices. Wasson's research, which spans cultures and continents, reveals a historical tapestry where psilocybin mushrooms were not only consumed but also venerated.

Psychoactive Rituals: The ritualistic use of psilocybin mushrooms in Mesoamerican cultures has been extensively documented by ethnomycologists like Terence McKenna in his book "Food of the Gods" (1992). McKenna hypothesizes that these substances were integral to various spiritual practices, including healing ceremonies, divinatory rituals, and as a means to commune with the divine or ancestral spirits. While empirical evidence from these ancient times is scarce, the persistence of such practices among indigenous communities, such as the Mazatecs in Oaxaca, provides a living testament to these ancient traditions.

Speculative Links in Early Christian Iconography: The Plaincourault Chapel Fresco

Psychedelic Hypotheses: The Plaincourault Chapel fresco, dating back to the 12th century in France, has become a focal point for speculative theories regarding the presence of psychedelics in early Christian art. John M. Allegro's controversial book "The Sacred Mushroom and the Cross" (1970) presents a hypothesis that the peculiar tree depicted in the fresco is symbolic of Amanita muscaria, a psychoactive mushroom. Allegro suggests that such iconography may be indicative of esoteric knowledge and the use of psychedelics within early Christian sects.

Controversial Interpretations: These interpretations are far from universally accepted, with many scholars critiquing Allegro's approach. Mark J. Bonta, in his review article published in the "Journal for the Study of Religion, Nature and Culture" (2007), presents a critical examination of these claims, highlighting the lack of direct textual or archaeological evidence to support the presence of psychoactive substances in early Christian practices. Bonta argues that such interpretations often rely on a subjective analysis of religious symbols and narratives, which can lead to an overextension of speculative theories. The debate surrounding the Plaincourault Chapel fresco exemplifies the challenges of interpreting historical and religious art, where the original intent and context may be obscured by the passage of time.

While the portrayal of psychoactive substances in ancient art and religious iconography opens a window into the possible psychoactive practices of the past, the interpretations are often speculative and subject to academic debate. As we continue to uncover and analyze these historical artifacts, they offer a tantalizing glimpse into the complex relationship between humans, psychoactive substances, and the pursuit of spiritual and artistic expression.

Psychedelia's Imprint on Art, Music, and Literature: A Cultural Renaissance

Psychedelics have not only influenced individual consciousness but have also left an indelible mark on the collective creative spirit, particularly in the realms of visual arts, music, and literature. These substances have acted as muses, inspiring a cultural renaissance that redefined the boundaries of perception and expression.

Visual Arts: A Portal to the Surreal

Surrealism and Beyond: The Surrealism movement, which flourished in the early 20th century, was founded by André Breton in his 1924 "Manifesto of Surrealism". Its ethos was to reconcile the contradictory states of dream and reality into an absolute reality, a 'super-reality'. Artists like Salvador Dali, René Magritte, and Max Ernst delved into the subconscious mind, drawing inspiration from the theories of Sigmund Freud. Dali's "The Persistence of Memory" (1931), with its melting clocks in a desolate landscape, is often interpreted as a representation of the fluidity of time—a concept that resonates with the altered perception of time in psychedelic experiences. Dali's meticulous technique and paradoxical images aimed to disrupt the viewer's conventional understanding of reality, much like the effect of psychedelic substances.

Psychedelic Art Movement: The Psychedelic Art movement exploded onto the scene in the mid-1960s, epitomized by the visually arresting works that emerged from the San Francisco Bay Area. Artists like Peter Max, with his cosmic 60s art, and Victor Moscoso, renowned for his neon-colored concert posters for bands like The Grateful Dead, defined the aesthetic of an era. Their art was not only reflective of the psychedelic experience but also became emblematic of the counterculture movement. The 1966 "Trips Festival" in San Francisco, for instance, featured psychedelic art and light shows that provided a sensory experience mirroring the effects of psychedelic drugs. This art form was not only confined to canvases but also translated into album covers, concert posters, and even clothing, becoming a visual lexicon for the cultural revolution of the time.

The "Trips Festival"

The "Trips Festival," held in San Francisco from January 21 to 23, 1966, stands as a seminal event in the history of the psychedelic movement and the counterculture of the 1960s. Orchestrated by Stewart Brand, Ken Kesey, and the Merry Pranksters, the festival was a convergence of multimedia, music, and the psychedelic experience, drawing a crowd of around 10,000 people over its three-day duration.

Location and Setup: The festival took place at the Longshoremen's Hall, a two-story venue in San Francisco. The main floor was transformed into a multisensory environment. It featured innovative lighting techniques, including strobe lights and liquid light shows, which involved the projection of brightly colored, swirling patterns created by shining light through a mixture of oil and colored water, a technique pioneered by artists like Bill Ham.

Musical Performances: Music was a central element of the festival, with performances by notable psychedelic rock bands of the time. The Grateful Dead, then known as The Warlocks, and Big Brother and the Holding Company, featuring Janis Joplin, were among the prominent acts. Their music, characterized by extended improvisations and experimental sounds, complemented the psychedelic atmosphere.

Interactive Elements: Ken Kesey and the Merry Pranksters, known for their cross-country trips in a psychedelically painted school bus named "Further," contributed to the festival's interactive nature. They engaged the audience in games and spontaneous performances, blurring the lines between performers and spectators. The festival also featured avant-garde dance performances and experimental films, adding layers to the sensory experience.

Cultural Impact: The "Trips Festival" is often credited with catalyzing the Summer of Love in 1967, as it was one of the first events to bring the counterculture and psychedelic movement into the public eye on a large scale. It highlighted the potential of music and multimedia art to create immersive environments that mirrored and enhanced the effects of psychedelic substances, paving the way for future music festivals and "happenings" that defined the era.

In summary, the "Trips Festival" was a landmark event that encapsulated the spirit of the 1960s counterculture, combining music, art, and community in a celebration of the psychedelic experience. Its legacy continues to influence cultural festivals and the integration of multimedia art in public events.

Music: Echoes of Altered Consciousness

The inception of psychedelic rock can be traced back to the early 1960s, with bands like The Byrds and 13th Floor Elevators. The Beatles' "Sgt. Pepper's Lonely Hearts Club Band" (1967) is often cited as a turning point in the genre, with its innovative use of studio effects, non-traditional instruments, and lyrical abstraction. Pink Floyd's "The Dark Side of the Moon" (1973) is another milestone, selling over 45 million copies worldwide. Its thematic exploration of mental illness, greed, conflict, and the passage of time was accentuated by pioneering sound effects and studio experimentation, creating a soundscape that mirrored the hallucinogenic experience.

Pink Floyd's "Comfortably Numb", from their album "The Wall" (1979), features guitar solos that are often described as one of the greatest in rock history. The song's lyrics, which describe a detached, dreamlike state, resonate with the dissociative effects of psychedelics.

Literature: A Chronicle of Psychedelic Journeys

Aldous Huxley's "The Doors of Perception" details his experiences with mescaline, ingested under the supervision of a psychiatrist in May 1953. Huxley's account, which explores the vivid visual sensations and philosophical reflections elicited by the substance, was a seminal work in articulating the potential of psychedelics to expand consciousness. The title itself, borrowed from a line by poet William Blake, suggests that psychedelics can unlock new realms of perception.

The Beat Generation, a literary movement of the 1950s and 60s, often featured drug use as a means of achieving altered states of consciousness. Hunter S. Thompson's "Fear and Loathing in Las Vegas" (1971) is a prime example, combining fact and fiction in a narrative that explores the American Dream through the lens of a psychedelic trip. Jack Kerouac's "On the Road" (1957), while not explicitly focused on psychedelics, captures the spirit of freedom and non-conformity that characterized the Beat Generation and the subsequent psychedelic era.

The impact of psychedelics on art, music, and literature is a testament to their profound influence on human creativity and cultural evolution. From the dreamscapes of surrealism to the sonic explorations of psychedelic rock and through the introspective literary journeys, these substances have expanded the horizons of artistic expression, challenging and redefining the boundaries of perception.

Psychedelic Culture of the 1960s and 1970s: An Era of Awakening and Resistance

The 1960s and 1970s were not just decades; they were a state of mind, a cultural revolution underpinned by a quest for deeper meaning and a rebellion against the status quo. Psychedelics, such as psilocybin, LSD, and mescaline, became not just substances but symbols—emblems of an awakening, a collective urge for self-discovery, and a repudiation of conventional norms.

The Psychedelic-Infused Counterculture Movement

The 1960s counterculture movement was a profound societal shift that questioned authority and sought personal and societal transformation.

Psychedelics, such as LSD and psilocybin, became emblematic of this rebellion. These substances believed, to expand consciousness and enhance creativity, contrasted sharply with the conservative values of post-World War II society. Harvard University's Dr. Timothy Leary became a key figure in this movement. His early studies, such as the Concord Prison Experiment (1961-1963) and the Marsh Chapel Experiment (1962), initially focused on the potential therapeutic effects of psilocybin. However, his public advocacy for LSD use, which led to his dismissal from Harvard in 1963, positioned him as a counterculture icon. The Concord Prison Experiment aimed to reduce recidivism rates among inmates through psilocybin-assisted psychotherapy. Although initial reports suggested a significant reduction in recidivism, later reviews, such as the follow-up study by Rick Doblin in 1998, highlighted methodological flaws and found no significant differences.

The Woodstock Music Festival, held in August 1969 in Bethel, New York, drew an estimated crowd of 400,000 people. It featured iconic performances from artists like Jimi Hendrix, Janis Joplin, and The Who and became a symbol of the counterculture era, celebrated in the 1970 documentary film "Woodstock." The Summer of Love in 1967 in San Francisco's Haight-Ashbury district is another hallmark of the era. It drew as many as 100,000 people, predominantly young adults, who converged to create a community based on shared values of peace, love, and an open exploration of psychedelics. This event was pivotal in popularizing the counterculture movement and was documented in works like "The Electric Kool-Aid Acid Test" by Tom Wolfe (1968).

The Concord Prison Experiment (1961-1963)

The Concord Prison Experiment was an early study conducted by Dr. Timothy Leary and his colleagues at Harvard University to investigate the potential of psilocybin-assisted psychotherapy in reducing recidivism rates among inmates at Concord State Prison. The study was based on the hypothesis that psilocybin, a psychoactive compound found in certain species of mushrooms, could induce profound transformative experiences that might lead to behavior change.

Design and Methodology: The study involved the administration of psilocybin to 36 prisoners who had volunteered to participate. These volunteers were given a single high dose of psilocybin in a session that was intended to mimic a religious or mystical experience. The sessions were guided by trained personnel who provided support and reassurance to the participants.

Alongside the psilocybin sessions, the participants engaged in group therapy and discussions designed to help them integrate their experiences into their daily lives.

Initial Results: The initial findings suggested that there was a significant reduction in recidivism rates among the participants.

Reports indicated that only 25% of the participants returned to prison within six months of release, compared to the expected recidivism rate of 60% based on historical data for similar cohorts.

Subsequent Reviews and Criticism: Despite the initial positive results, the study faced criticism for methodological flaws. These included the lack of a control group, potential biases in the selection of participants, and the absence of long-term follow-up.

A retrospective analysis by Rick Doblin in 1998 found that the initial reduction in recidivism rates was not sustained over time, and there was no significant difference compared to non-participants.

The study's design and the optimistic interpretations of its results have since been viewed as examples of the challenges in controlling for variables in psychedelic research.

The Marsh Chapel Experiment (1962), also known as the "Good Friday Experiment"

The Marsh Chapel Experiment was a landmark study conducted by Walter Pahnke as part of his doctoral dissertation at Harvard University under the supervision of Dr. Timothy Leary. The study sought to investigate whether psilocybin could induce mystical experiences in religiously predisposed individuals.

Design and Methodology: The experiment took place on Good Friday at Marsh Chapel in Boston, with the participation of 20 theological seminary students.

The students were divided into two groups: 10 received a capsule containing 30 milligrams of psilocybin, and 10 received a placebo capsule with niacin, which can produce physiological sensations similar to psilocybin but without the psychoactive effects.

The participants were unaware of which substance they had received.

The experiment was conducted during a traditional Good Friday service to provide a religious setting that might enhance the potential for mystical experiences.

Results: The majority of the participants who received psilocybin reported profound religious or mystical experiences characterized by a sense of unity, transcendence of time and space, and deep spiritual significance.

The experiences were rated by Pahnke as being similar to spontaneously occurring mystical experiences described in religious literature.

In contrast, the placebo group reported significantly fewer such experiences.

A long-term follow-up study conducted by Rick Doblin in 1991 found that the participants who received psilocybin still considered their experience to be spiritually significant and personally meaningful two decades later.

Significance and Legacy: The Marsh Chapel Experiment is considered one of the earliest controlled studies demonstrating the capacity of psychedelics to induce mystical experiences in a religious context. It laid the groundwork for subsequent research exploring the interplay between psychedelics, spirituality, and therapy.

Both studies, despite their limitations, played pivotal roles in the early exploration of psychedelics' potential for inducing profound psychological and spiritual transformations. They have informed modern psychedelic research, which has evolved with more rigorous methodologies and ethical standards.

The "Summer of Love"

The Summer of Love in 1967 was a pivotal moment in the counterculture movement, characterized by an influx of young people to the Haight-Ashbury neighborhood of San Francisco. It was a phenomenon rooted in the ideals of peace, love, and communal living, and it left a lasting impact on American culture, politics, and the arts.

The Summer of Love had its roots in the evolving counterculture of the 1960s, with influences ranging from the civil rights movement and anti-Vietnam War protests to the burgeoning interest in Eastern spirituality and the psychedelic experience. The "Trips Festival" and other earlier gatherings helped to lay the groundwork for this cultural explosion.

Haight-Ashbury became the epicenter of the Summer of Love due to its affordable housing and the growing presence of artists, musicians, and radical thinkers. It attracted young people from all over the country, drawn by the promise of a new way of living, free from the constraints of mainstream society. At its peak, it is estimated that around 100,000 individuals converged in the neighborhood.

Music played a crucial role in the Summer of Love, with the San Francisco Sound being at the forefront. Bands like The Grateful Dead, Jefferson Airplane, and Janis Joplin's Big Brother and the Holding Company became icons of the era. The Monterey Pop Festival in June 1967, featuring performances by Jimi Hendrix, The Who, and Ravi Shankar, was a significant event that highlighted the cultural and musical diversity of the movement.

The Diggers, an anarchist street theater group, were influential in shaping the ethos of the Summer of Love. They organized free food distributions, free stores, and street theater events, promoting a vision of society based on sharing and community. Their activities challenged the commercialization of the counterculture and promoted an ethos of self-sufficiency and mutual aid.

Media and Commercialization: The media played a dual role in the Summer of Love. On one hand, it helped to spread the message of peace and love, drawing more young people to San Francisco. On the other hand, it contributed to the commercialization of the movement, with mainstream society co-opting and commodifying its symbols and ideals. This led to tensions within the counterculture between those seeking to preserve its authenticity and those embracing its mainstream appeal.

The Summer of Love left a lasting legacy in American culture. It influenced fashion, music, and art, and its ideals of peace, love, and community continue to resonate. It also had a significant impact on social and political movements, contributing to the growing awareness of environmental issues, gender equality, and LGBTQ+ rights.

The Summer of Love remains a symbol of a transformative moment in history when a generation dared to envision a different way of living and being in the world. Its impact continues to be felt in the pursuit of social justice, environmental sustainability, and the quest for a more inclusive and compassionate society.

Woodstock

The Woodstock Music and Art Fair, commonly referred to simply as "Woodstock," was a landmark event not just in music history but also as a cultural touchstone for the 1960s counterculture movement. Its impact was far-reaching, resonating with themes of peace, love, and music.

Dr. Isabella Rodriguez

Background and Planning: Woodstock was originally conceived by four young men: Joel Rosenman, John Roberts, Artie Kornfeld, and Mike Lang. Their initial idea was to create a recording studio in Woodstock, New York, a town known for its artist community and as a retreat for musicians such as Bob Dylan.

To finance this studio, they planned a two-day rock concert for 50,000 people. However, the event evolved far beyond their expectations.

Location and Infrastructure: After several changes in location and facing opposition from locals, the organizers secured Max Yasgur's dairy farm in Bethel, New York, just over 40 miles from the town of Woodstock.

The festival site had to be prepared in a hurry, and as the crowds began to arrive, the fences meant to secure the area were never completed, making it a free concert for many attendees.

The Festival: Woodstock took place from August 15 to 18, 1969. The dates extended beyond the planned timeframe due to delays and extended performances.

Despite the rain, food shortages, and the logistical nightmare of accommodating an unexpected number of people (estimates range from 400,000 to half a million), the festival maintained a largely peaceful and positive atmosphere.

The iconic opening ceremony featured Swami Satchidananda, who set the tone with a message of peace and harmony.

Performances and Musicians: Woodstock featured 32 acts, encompassing a wide range of musical genres. Notable performers included Richie Havens, Joan Baez, Janis Joplin, The Who, Jefferson Airplane, and Crosby, Stills, Nash & Young.

Jimi Hendrix's closing performance, which included his famous rendition of "The Star-Spangled Banner," remains one of the most celebrated moments in rock history.

Cultural Impact: Woodstock became a symbol of the 1960s counterculture movement, epitomizing the era's spirit of peace, love, music, and resistance to the Vietnam War.

It showcased the power of music to unite people and became a blueprint for future music festivals.

The "Woodstock Generation" became a term used to describe those who embrace the ideals of peace, love, and community.

Legacy and Media: The documentary film "Woodstock," released in 1970, played a significant role in cementing the festival's legendary status. It won the Academy Award for Best Documentary Feature and provided those who weren't there a glimpse into the event's atmosphere.

The soundtrack of the film, featuring live performances from the festival, was also a commercial success.

Woodstock remains a defining moment of the 20th century, symbolizing the peak of the 1960s counterculture movement and illustrating the unifying power of music and collective experience.

Key Figures: Prophets of a Psychedelic Age

Timothy Leary - The Psychedelic Evangelist: Timothy Leary's advocacy for psychedelics was both transformative and controversial. After his dismissal from Harvard, Leary continued his advocacy, becoming a central figure in the psychedelic movement. His slogan, "Turn on, tune in, drop out," first coined at the Human Be-In event in San Francisco in 1967, became synonymous with the counterculture movement. Leary's research included studies like the Harvard Psilocybin Project, which aimed to understand the effects of psilocybin on human consciousness. However, Leary's approach and the uncontrolled nature of some of his experiments attracted criticism and were part of the reason for the increased governmental regulation of these substances.

Ram Dass - From Academic to Spiritual Teacher: Richard Alpert's transformation into Ram Dass followed his experimentation with psychedelics alongside Leary. His journey to India in 1967 and his subsequent tutelage under the Hindu guru Neem Karoli Baba marked a significant shift from academic to spiritual teacher. His 1971 book "Be Here Now" became a seminal work in the spiritual and psychedelic communities. The book is not just a narrative of his transformation but a compilation of various spiritual teachings and practices. It has sold over 2 million copies worldwide and continues to influence spiritual seekers and advocates of psychedelics' transformative potential.

The psychedelic culture of the 1960s and 1970s was far more than a mere period of drug experimentation. It was a collective quest for deeper meaning, a crusade against the mechanistic worldview, and a rebirth of spiritual and creative expression.

Psilocybin's Ripple Effect in Popular Culture: From Screen to Soundtrack to Story

Psilocybin and psychedelics at large have cast a long, colorful shadow over popular culture, influencing a variety of artistic domains. From the flickering screens of cinemas to the rhythmic pulses of music and the contemplative realm of literature, these substances have acted as muses, sparking creativity, introspection, and sometimes controversy.

Cinematic Explorations of the Psychedelic Experience

"Altered States" (1980): Directed by Ken Russell and written by Paddy Chayefsky, based on his novel of the same name, "Altered States" is a pioneering film in its portrayal of psychedelic experiences. The protagonist, Dr. Edward Jessup (played by William Hurt in his film debut), is a university professor who studies abnormal psychology and the origins of consciousness. His experiments involve sensory deprivation tanks and the ingestion of powerful hallucinogens resembling the Amazonian psychedelic brew Ayahuasca. The special effects in the film were groundbreaking for their time, especially the sequences depicting Jessup's hallucinations, which involve complex visual patterns and biological transformations. The film's portrayal of altered states of consciousness through a combination of sound, editing, and visual effects aimed to immerse the viewer in the protagonist's psychedelic journey. While it received mixed reviews from critics, it has since gained a cult following and is noted for its ambitious and, at times, disturbing visualizations of the inner workings of the mind.

"Enter the Void" (2009): Gaspar Noé's "Enter the Void" is a cinematic exploration of life, death, and the afterlife through a psychedelic lens. The story follows Oscar, an American drug dealer living in Tokyo, who is shot and killed during a drug bust. The film then takes the viewer on a journey through Oscar's post-death experience, heavily influenced by the Tibetan Book of the Dead, a Buddhist text that describes the stages of death and rebirth. The narrative structure of the film mimics the disorientation and non-linearity of a psychedelic trip, with vivid neon-lit visuals and a first-person perspective that drifts through scenes and memories. The film's explicit and unfiltered portrayal of drug use, sex, and violence, coupled with its unique visual style, make it a polarizing yet impactful representation of altered states of consciousness.

In more recent cinematic ventures, the 2019 film "Midsommar," directed by Ari Aster, provides a contemporary take on the use of psychedelics within the narrative. The film portrays a group of friends who travel to Sweden for a rural mid-summer festival that quickly descends into a disturbing pagan cult ritual. Psychedelics, in the form of naturally occurring substances, play a crucial role in the film, acting as a catalyst for the main character's emotional journey and the disorienting and often terrifying events that unfold. The visuals of 'Midsommar' are saturated with bright colors and kaleidoscopic patterns, attempting to mimic the visual distortions experienced during a psychedelic trip. While not a central focus, the film's use of psychedelics underscores its themes of grief, transformation, and the search for belonging.

Musical Anthems and Inspirations

The Beatles' Psychedelic Influence: "Lucy in the Sky with Diamonds," from the album "Sgt. Pepper's Lonely Hearts Club Band" (1967), is one of The Beatles' most famous songs associated with psychedelic culture. The album marked a significant shift in the band's musical style, incorporating elements of psychedelia, Eastern music, and innovative studio techniques. Producer George Martin played a crucial role in realizing the band's creative vision, utilizing techniques such as tape loops, varispeed, and reversed recordings to create a groundbreaking soundscape. "Sgt. Pepper's Lonely Hearts Club Band" was an immediate commercial and critical success, spending 27 weeks at the top of the UK Albums Chart and 15 weeks at number one in the US. It won four Grammy Awards in 1968, including Album of the Year, the first rock LP to receive this honor.

Modern Musical Continuations: Tame Impala, the psychedelic music project of Australian musician Kevin Parker, has been influential in reviving and reinterpreting the psychedelic sound for a modern audience. Albums like "Lonerism" (2012) and "Currents" (2015) have received critical acclaim for their fusion of psychedelic rock with electronic and pop elements. Tame Impala's music often features themes of introspection, isolation, and the nature of reality, paralleling the introspective qualities of a psychedelic experience. MGMT, an American band formed by Benjamin Goldwasser and Andrew VanWyngarden, gained prominence with their 2007 debut album "Oracular Spectacular." The album's single "Time to Pretend" is a satirical take on the rockstar lifestyle, and its accompanying music video features psychedelic visuals. MGMT's sound has evolved over the years, but their music continues to incorporate psychedelic themes and sonic textures.

Literary Journeys Through the Psychedelic Landscape

Michael Pollan's "How to Change Your Mind": Published in 2018, "How to Change Your Mind" delves into the renaissance of psychedelic research after decades of stigma and legal restrictions. Pollan explores the therapeutic potential of substances like LSD, psilocybin, and MDMA, covering their history, the cultural context that led to their demonization, and the recent resurgence of scientific interest in their potential to treat conditions like depression, addiction and end-of-life anxiety. The book highlights research from institutions like Johns Hopkins University, where studies have shown significant reductions in depression and anxiety symptoms in cancer patients following psilocybin-assisted therapy. For example, a study published in the "Journal of Psychopharmacology" in 2016 reported that psilocybin produced substantial and sustained decreases in depression and anxiety in patients with life-threatening cancer diagnoses, with about 80% of participants continuing to show clinically significant decreases in both conditions six months after treatment. Pollan also narrates his personal experiences with psychedelics, providing an introspective and nuanced perspective on their transformative potential. The book has been influential in bringing balanced and well-researched discussions of psychedelics to a broader audience, contributing to the growing interest in their therapeutic possibilities.

"The Immortality Key: The Secret History of the Religion with No Name " by Brian C. Muraresku, published in 2020, delves into the hypothesis that psychedelic substances have played a pivotal role in the spiritual practices of ancient civilizations. Muraresku presents an intriguing narrative backed by archaeological evidence and historical texts, suggesting that psychedelics may have influenced early Christian rituals and other religious ceremonies. While the book is more speculative than Pollan's, it expands the conversation around psychedelics' historical and cultural significance."

Psilocybin's influence on popular culture is indelible and multifaceted. It has been a source of inspiration and exploration across various artistic mediums, reflecting society's fascination with the boundaries of consciousness and the human experience.

Conclusion

The influence of psilocybin mushrooms winds through diverse facets of culture, weaving a complex tapestry that transcends singular definition. In rituals and folklore, they opened portals to spiritual awakening. In music and art, they dissolved barriers, inspiring unbridled creativity. Through cautionary tales and stigmas, they became symbols of youthful defiance and political control.

Yet their enduring cultural presence testifies to humanity's age-old fascination with these mushrooms' singular ability to unfetter consciousness. In some moments of history, this power was embraced, even venerated, while in others, it was demonized and suppressed. But the mushroom itself remains an emissary that continues to shape our collective imagination, insight, and understanding.

As psilocybin glides into the spotlight once more, its cultural impact will again reshape and evolve based on the temperaments of the era. Yet some legacies persist regardless of the cultural milieu - things like reverence for nature's gifts, faith in humanity's potential for growth, and trust in the sanctity of inner realms that transcend any single historical moment. In this light, the psilocybin mushroom stands as a reminder that creation is infinitely more complex, beautiful and loving than our transient cultures can sometimes reflect.

CHAPTER 7: The Evolution of Psilocybin in Popular Media

Psilocybin's Surprising Media Evolution from Taboo to Trendsetter.

- Streaming series shift psilocybin's portrayal
- Podcasts influence public perception
- Social media's role in policy change

In the rapidly evolving landscape of popular media, psilocybin mushrooms have emerged from the shadows of taboos to feature prominently in various formats. This chapter examines the portrayal of psilocybin across streaming services, podcasts, and social media, scrutinizing its influence on public opinion and policy-making.

Psilocybin's Portrayal in Streaming Series

In the realm of streaming series, the portrayal of psilocybin has undergone a significant transformation. The early 2000s often saw psilocybin depicted humorously or as a warning against drug use. However, as societal attitudes toward mental health and substance use have progressed, so too has the representation of psilocybin on screen. Contemporary series are exploring its therapeutic potential and the profound personal discoveries it can catalyze, reflecting a broader cultural shift in our understanding of psychedelics.

Context in Streaming Media

Early representations of psilocybin in series like "That '70s Show" or "Entourage" often used it as a plot device for humor or to showcase the perils of drug use. These portrayals mirrored the cautionary stance prevalent in society during the time, influenced by the War on Drugs narrative.

However, there has been a discernible shift in recent years, with streaming platforms now presenting more balanced and researched perspectives on psilocybin, aligning with changing societal views and scientific discoveries.

Show "The Midnight Gospel" blended entertainment with deep conversations about life, death, and substances like psilocybin in a way that's both accessible and thought-provoking.

"Nine Perfect Strangers" delves into the healing journeys of its characters, highlighting psilocybin's use in a therapeutic setting.

"Goop Lab", despite facing criticism for its approach to wellness, has episodes that discuss the potential benefits of psychedelics, including psilocybin, featuring interviews with experts and users.

"Hamilton's Pharmacopeia" offers a documentary-style look at psychedelics, presenting the chemistry, history, and cultural impact of substances like psilocybin.

"The Mind, Explained" docuseries explores the intricacies of the brain and includes an episode on psychedelics, which presents both the historical use of psilocybin and current research findings. Such shows often include commentary from neuroscientists and psychologists, providing viewers with credible information.

These shows and others have been noted for their educational value and their role in changing the conversation around psychedelics.

Engagement with Scientific Community

Some series have prompted discussions within the scientific community itself, as seen with the release of Netflix's "How to Change Your Mind." Conversations around such series can even influence the direction of future research, highlighting the reciprocal relationship between media and science.

As these shows reach a global audience, they serve an educational purpose, often prompting viewers to seek out additional information from scientific journals and advocacy organizations. For example, viewership spikes have been linked to increased web traffic to sites like MAPS and the Psychedelic Science Review.

Research institutions sometimes conduct surveys following the release of series with drug-related content to gauge changes in public perception. These surveys can provide insights into the effectiveness of media in altering societal views on substances like psilocybin.

The evolution of psilocybin's portrayal in streaming series from a comedic trope to a subject of therapeutic exploration mirrors a larger societal shift towards accepting and understanding psychedelics. As streaming content continues to shape cultural discourse, the nuanced narratives of psilocybin use in shows like "Nine Perfect Strangers" and "Goop Lab" play a pivotal role in fostering a more informed and open dialogue. These portrayals encourage viewers to consider the complex realities of psychedelic substances beyond the stigma, possibly paving the way for more progressive drug policies and greater support for psychedelic research.

Psilocybin Discussions in Podcasts

Podcasts have become a pivotal platform for disseminating information and fostering discussions on a plethora of subjects, including the nuanced world of psilocybin. Renowned podcasts such as "The Joe Rogan Experience" and "The Tim Ferriss Show" are prime examples of how these digital conversations can educate and influence public opinion on psychedelics. By inviting experts to discuss the latest research, therapeutic applications, and personal anecdotes, these podcasts are instrumental in demystifying psilocybin and expanding its dialogue to a wider audience.

Educational Platforms and Expert Discussions

"The Joe Rogan Experience" often features scientists like Paul Stamets and other figures who share insights on the science, cultural significance, and personal experiences with psilocybin.

"The Tim Ferriss Show" delves into the potential of psychedelics for mental health, with Ferriss often discussing his own experiences and supporting psychedelic research initiatives.

These platforms serve as a bridge between the scientific community and the general public, providing a space for experts to disseminate their findings and for listeners to engage with complex topics in an accessible format.

Podcasts have become a pivotal educational tool, with episodes dedicated to psychedelics often going viral, significantly widening the audience for psychedelic education. Programs like "Psychedelics Today" focus exclusively on the subject, discussing everything from the latest scientific research to personal narratives and policy issues.

Celebrities like Mike Tyson on his podcast "Hotboxin' with Mike Tyson" openly discuss their transformative experiences with psychedelics, including psilocybin. Such endorsements can have a profound influence on public opinion, given their wide reach and the personal connection fans feel with these figures.

The Ripple Effect on Listeners

Listeners report not only a spike in interest but also a change in attitudes and behaviors regarding health and wellness practices. For example, after engaging with podcast content on psilocybin, some listeners have been documented seeking out legal psychedelic therapy sessions or participating in university-led research studies.

Research institutions have begun to analyze the impact of these podcasts by tracking changes in public opinion pre- and post-exposure to podcast episodes featuring psilocybin discussions. Such data-driven assessments are crucial for understanding the educational impact of these media platforms.

Podcasts are also playing a role in advocacy efforts, as listeners become more informed and motivated to engage in policy dialogue. For instance, organizations like MAPS have noted an uptick in donations and volunteerism correlating with podcast feature timings, suggesting a direct influence on public engagement with psychedelic advocacy and policy reform.

Podcasts have emerged as a significant force in shaping public discourse on psilocybin, transcending traditional barriers to education and discussion on psychedelics. By bringing expert voices to the forefront and fostering a conversational approach to complex topics, they contribute to an informed and open-minded public ready to engage with the multifaceted world of psilocybin. As these discussions continue to ripple through society, they hold the potential to influence not only individual perspectives but also the broader cultural and regulatory landscapes surrounding psychedelics.

Conclusion

The portrayal of psilocybin in popular media has undergone a remarkable transformation, reflecting changing societal attitudes and the relentless march of scientific progress. From caricatures of psychedelic escapism to nuanced explorations of its therapeutic potential, mainstream media representations have brought psilocybin out of the shadows and into the global spotlight.

No longer confined to sensationalism or stereotypes, today's nuanced portrayals are shaping perceptions and propelling advocacy. Streaming series with their normalizing lens, podcasts with their candid discussions, and social media with its boundless reach collectively scaffold a more informed and science-backed narrative.

Yet the story is far from over. As research continues apace and cultural narratives keep evolving, so too will media representations keep pace, either leading or mirroring shifts in mainstream consciousness. The modern information landscape, for all its polarizing pitfalls, allows the psilocybin conversation to spread unhindered, illuminating its role in mental health, creativity, and the enduring search for existential meaning.

CHAPTER 8: Psilocybin and the Brain

Psilocybin induces its effects by interacting with the brain's serotonin receptors.

- Neurological mechanisms of action
- Changes in brain activity and connectivity
- Long-term neurological effects

Psilocybin, a naturally occurring psychedelic compound, has fascinated both scientists and the public for its profound effects on the human brain and consciousness. Central to its impact is the interaction with serotonin receptors, particularly the 5-HT2A receptor, which plays a pivotal role in the compound's psychoactive effects. The way psilocybin modulates brain activity and connectivity has far-reaching implications not only for our understanding of consciousness but also for its potential therapeutic applications.

Decoding the Psychoactive Journey: The Role of Psilocybin and Serotonin Receptors

Psilocybin initiates a complex biochemical dance within the human brain, leading to profound alterations in consciousness and perception. Its mechanism of action is a compelling subject of scientific inquiry, providing insights into the intricate workings of our neural pathways.

The Chemical Transformation: Psilocybin to Psilocin

Psilocybin, the prodrug found in psychedelic mushrooms, undergoes a chemical transformation within the human body, converting into psilocin, its active form. This process is mediated by the liver enzyme alkaline phosphatase, which removes a phosphate group from psilocybin, converting it into psilocin. This dephosphorylation is a necessary step for the psychoactive effects to manifest, as psilocin can cross the blood-brain barrier, whereas psilocybin cannot.

The structural similarity of psilocin to serotonin (5-hydroxytryptamine or 5-HT) is noteworthy. Both molecules share an indole ring, which is a common structure found in many neurotransmitters and is thought to be crucial for binding to serotonin receptors in the brain. This resemblance allows psilocin to mimic serotonin and bind to its receptors, setting off a cascade of neurochemical reactions that underlie the psychedelic experience.

The Interaction with Serotonin Receptors

Psilocin's primary interaction is with the serotonin (5-HT) receptors, especially the 5-HT2A subtype. These receptors are found in high densities in key brain regions associated with cognition, perception, and the regulation of mood, such as the prefrontal cortex and the thalamus.

Activation of the 5-HT2A receptors by psilocin triggers a complex signaling cascade. This activation has been shown to lead to an increase in glutamate release, a neurotransmitter responsible for neural activation. Consequently, this can result in heightened neuronal activity, altered cognition, and changes in perception. It's also been suggested that the activation of these receptors leads to the suppression of the brain's default mode network (DMN), a network of interacting brain regions known to have activity highly correlated with each other and thought to be involved in self-referential thought processes.

The Binding Affinity of Psilocin to 5-HT2A Receptors

Psilocin's high binding affinity for the 5-HT2A receptor is a crucial aspect of its psychoactive profile. Binding affinity is a quantifiable measure of how strongly a molecule, like psilocin, binds to a specific receptor. This high affinity means that psilocin readily attaches to and activates the 5-HT2A receptor, a key trigger for its psychedelic effects.

The selectivity of psilocin for 5-HT2A receptors is significant because it largely determines the character and intensity of the psychedelic experience. While psilocin does interact with other serotonin receptors, such as 5-HT1A and 5-HT2C, its effects on the 5-HT2A receptor are particularly potent and central to its mind-altering capabilities.

The binding of psilocin to the 5-HT2A receptor initiates a sequence of molecular events that alter the receptor's conformation. This structural change triggers a cascade of intracellular signaling, which modifies the way neurons communicate with each other. These changes in neuronal firing patterns are what underlie the profound alterations in perception, thought, and emotion characteristic of a psychedelic experience.

The Cascade of Psychoactive Effects

The alteration of perception is one of the most notable effects of psilocybin. Users often report enhanced visual and auditory experiences, including vivid hallucinations and synesthesia – a blending of the senses where, for example, one might "see" sounds or "hear" colors. Additionally, psilocybin can distort one's sense of time, making moments feel elongated.

Emotionally, psilocybin can act as an amplifier, intensifying the user's current emotional state. It can elicit feelings of euphoria, interconnectedness, and spiritual experiences, but it can also provoke anxiety, fear, and dysphoria. The "set and setting" – the user's mindset and the physical and social environment in which they consume psilocybin – play crucial roles in shaping the experience.

Furthermore, psilocybin is being investigated for its potential in treating substance use disorders, including alcohol and tobacco dependence. Preliminary studies have shown promising results, with some participants maintaining prolonged periods of abstinence post-treatment.

In one of the more recent and notable studies, published in the "New England Journal of Medicine" on November 3, 2022, researchers conducted a phase 2, double-blind, randomized controlled trial comparing psilocybin with escitalopram, a standard antidepressant, in treating major depressive disorder. The study involved 59 participants who received either two doses of 25 mg of psilocybin and daily placebo capsules or two doses of 1 mg of psilocybin and daily escitalopram capsules over a 6-week period. The primary measure was the change in the Quick Inventory of Depressive Symptomatology–Self-Report (QIDS-SR-16) scores. While the reduction in depressive symptoms was not statistically significantly different between the groups, the findings highlighted the potential of psilocybin as a treatment for depression, with the advantage of requiring fewer treatment sessions compared to traditional antidepressants.

The psychoactive properties of psilocybin, facilitated through its conversion to psilocin and subsequent interaction with serotonin receptors, present a rich field of study. As the scientific community continues to explore this fascinating compound, the future may unveil even deeper insights into the mind-altering journey initiated by psilocybin.

Navigating the Mind: The Impact of Psilocybin on Key Brain Regions

Psilocybin's influence extends far beyond its initial interaction with serotonin receptors. As it courses through the brain, psilocybin leaves its mark on several critical regions, each responsible for fundamental aspects of our perception, behavior, and emotion. The prefrontal cortex, hippocampus, and amygdala, in particular, are significantly affected, leading to the profound and often transformative experiences reported by those who ingest psilocybin.

The Prefrontal Cortex: Seat of Complex Behavior

The prefrontal cortex is a region of the brain that plays a fundamental role in the orchestration of thoughts and actions in accordance with internal goals. It is the cerebral cortex that covers the front part of the frontal lobe. This brain region has been implicated in planning complex cognitive behavior, personality expression, decision-making, and moderating social behavior. It is involved in our higher cognitive functions, including memory, attention, and inhibitory control.

Psilocybin's effects on the prefrontal cortex have been the subject of intense research. One landmark study published in the "Proceedings of the National Academy of Sciences" in 2012 used functional magnetic resonance imaging (fMRI) to show that psilocybin decreases cerebral blood flow in the prefrontal cortex. This reduction in blood flow and activity could underlie the altered state of consciousness known as 'ego dissolution,' where the sense of self becomes less distinct and the boundaries between the self and the world blur.

The potential therapeutic implications of this effect are substantial. By dampening the activity of an overactive prefrontal cortex, psilocybin might alleviate symptoms of mental health disorders such as depression and anxiety. It's hypothesized that the rigid thought patterns characteristic of these disorders are disrupted, allowing for a psychological reset.

The Hippocampus: The Heart of Memory and Navigation

The hippocampus is a small, curved formation in the brain that plays an important role in the limbic system. It's involved in the formation of new memories and is also associated with learning and emotions. Given its role in memory formation and contextualization, alterations in hippocampal function can significantly affect how we perceive and interact with the world around us.

Research has shown that psilocybin can influence the functioning of the hippocampus. A study published in the "Journal of Psychopharmacology" in 2018 suggested that psilocybin might induce hippocampal neurogenesis—the growth and development of nervous tissue. This is of particular interest for treating conditions like PTSD, where the ability to form new, positive memories and diminish the impact of traumatic ones could be therapeutic.

The implications of this research are profound. If psilocybin can indeed promote hippocampal neurogenesis, it could be harnessed to aid recovery from neurological injuries or diseases that affect memory, such as Alzheimer's disease. However, more research is needed to understand the mechanisms by which psilocybin affects the hippocampus and to explore its therapeutic potential.

The Amygdala: Processing Emotions and Fears

The amygdala is an almond-shaped set of neurons located deep in the brain's medial temporal lobe. It plays a key role in the processing of emotions, especially those related to survival instincts like fear. Given its central role in emotional processing, the amygdala is a focal point in the study of the effects of psychedelics like psilocybin.

One study published in the journal "Neuropsychopharmacology" in 2016 investigated the effects of psilocybin on amygdala reactivity. The researchers found that a single dose of psilocybin decreased amygdala reactivity to negative stimuli, such as fearful faces. This decrease in reactivity was correlated with an increase in positive mood in study participants.

The potential long-term impacts of these immediate effects are an exciting avenue of research. By reducing the amygdala's reactivity to negative stimuli, psilocybin might foster long-term emotional resilience. This could be particularly beneficial for individuals with anxiety disorders, including PTSD, where the amygdala's heightened response to fear and threat can be debilitating. Psilocybin's ability to induce a state of emotional openness might also facilitate therapeutic interventions as individuals become more receptive to confronting and working through traumatic memories.

The profound influence of psilocybin on the prefrontal cortex, hippocampus, and amygdala underlines its capacity to alter not just our immediate perception but potentially the very structure and function of our brains. As scientific inquiry delves deeper into these interactions, the potential for psilocybin as a catalyst for therapeutic change becomes increasingly evident, marking a new era in our approach to mental health treatment.

Brain Activity and Connectivity on Psilocybin

The enigmatic nature of psychedelic experiences has long intrigued both scientists and the public. Psilocybin, in particular, has been a focus of interest due to its profound effects on consciousness. With the advent of advanced neuroimaging techniques like functional magnetic resonance imaging (fMRI) and positron emission tomography (PET), researchers have begun to peel back the layers of mystery surrounding psilocybin's impact on the brain.

Brain Imaging Studies: Windows into the Psychedelic Brain

Brain imaging techniques such as functional magnetic resonance imaging (fMRI) and positron emission tomography (PET) have been instrumental in unraveling the effects of psilocybin on the brain. These techniques provide a dynamic view of the brain at work, offering insights into blood flow patterns (fMRI) and glucose metabolism (PET), which are proxies for neural activity.

One of the seminal studies in this area was published in the "British Journal of Psychiatry" in 2012. The researchers employed fMRI to investigate the brain activity of individuals under the influence of psilocybin. The study revealed a significant decrease in blood flow to regions such as the medial prefrontal cortex (mPFC) and the posterior cingulate cortex (PCC). These regions are part of the brain's "default mode network" (DMN), which is active during rest and involved in self-referential thought processes, such as daydreaming and self-reflection. The mPFC, in particular, is associated with self-consciousness and introspection. The decreased activity in these areas is thought to correspond with the phenomenon of "ego dissolution" commonly reported by individuals using psilocybin, where the sense of self becomes less distinct.

The implications of these findings are substantial. By dampening the activity of the DMN, psilocybin might help disrupt the over-engagement of these regions seen in conditions such as depression. This could alleviate the rumination and excessive self-focus characteristic of depressive states.

"Hyperconnected" Brain States: A Symphony of Synchrony

Psilocybin induces a unique state of "hyperconnectivity" in the brain, where regions that usually do not communicate directly begin to interact. This enhanced connectivity is believed to break down the normal communication barriers within the brain, potentially leading to the extraordinary perceptual and cognitive experiences associated with psychedelics.

One study that illustrates this increased connectivity was published in "The Journal of Neuroscience" in 2014. The researchers found that psilocybin led to synchronized activity across brain regions involved in different functions, such as vision, attention, movement, and hearing. This might explain synesthetic experiences reported by some users, such as "seeing" sounds or "hearing" colors. For instance, the study found increased cross-talk between the visual cortex and other parts of the brain, which could underlie the vivid visual hallucinations and altered perception of reality commonly reported during psychedelic experiences.

The therapeutic potential of this hyperconnected state is significant. By fostering novel connections and breaking down the habitual patterns of brain activity, psilocybin could facilitate a kind of "cognitive reset." This might explain the enduring changes in personality traits, such as increased openness and the profound shifts in perspective reported by many users. Such effects could be harnessed in therapeutic settings, particularly for conditions characterized by negative thought patterns and a sense of disconnection, including depression and anxiety disorders.

Brain imaging studies have significantly advanced our understanding of how psilocybin reshapes brain activity and connectivity. By revealing both the localized and network-wide changes that occur during a psychedelic experience, these studies not only demystify the biological underpinnings of psychedelia but also pave the way for new therapeutic applications that could revolutionize mental health treatment.

Implications for Consciousness and Perception

The profound alterations in consciousness elicited by psilocybin present a fascinating window into the malleable nature of human perception and the sense of self. The radical shifts experienced by individuals under the influence of this substance have been a subject of both scientific scrutiny and philosophical intrigue, pushing the boundaries of our understanding of the mind.

Altered Perception: A Multisensory Metamorphosis

Transformations Across Senses: Psilocybin is renowned for inducing changes in visual, auditory, and sensory perception. Common visual alterations include enhanced colors, geometric patterns, and visual distortions. Auditory changes may involve alterations in the perception of sounds and an enhanced ability to "visualize" music.

One study published in "Psychopharmacology" in 2011 demonstrated that psilocybin can induce synesthesia-like experiences in individuals who don't usually experience this phenomenon, suggesting a temporary re-wiring of sensory processing in the brain.

These perceptual changes are not mere hallucinations but are often accompanied by profound emotional and cognitive shifts, suggesting a deeper reconfiguration of how individuals process and interpret their environment.

Altered Sense of Self: The Dissolution and Rebirth of Ego

A hallmark of the psychedelic experience is a phenomenon often referred to as "ego dissolution," where the normal boundaries between the self and the external world become blurred. This can lead to a profound sense of unity or interconnectedness with others and the universe at large.

Research, such as a study published in the "Journal of Psychopharmacology" in 2016, has linked this experience of ego dissolution to decreases in activity within the default mode network, a brain network associated with self-referential thought processes.

The experience of ego dissolution has been suggested to have therapeutic potential, providing relief from the rigid self-narratives that characterize conditions like depression and anxiety, as evidenced by the growing body of research advocating for psychedelic-assisted therapy.

The implications of psilocybin-induced changes in consciousness are manifold, touching on the deepest philosophical questions about the nature of reality and self. The growing body of scientific literature is not only validating the subjective reports of psychedelic users but is also opening new avenues for understanding the human mind.

Long-term Neurological Effects

The enigmatic compound psilocybin doesn't just offer a transient escape from the ordinary; emerging research suggests it may catalyze long-term changes in brain structure and function, heralding potential benefits for neuroplasticity and cognition.

Neuroplasticity Benefits: A Renaissance in the Brain

Neuroplasticity, the brain's ability to reorganize itself by forming new neural connections, is at the heart of learning, memory, and recovery from brain injuries. Psilocybin, an active compound in magic mushrooms, has been shown to significantly influence this process.

A study published in the "International Journal of Molecular Sciences" in 2020 delved into the mechanisms of neuroplasticity induced by psychedelic compounds, including psilocybin. The researchers highlighted the role of these substances in promoting both neurogenesis and synaptogenesis, which are crucial for neural repair and the development of new learning pathways. The study emphasized that psilocybin facilitates the growth of new neurons (neurogenesis) and enhances the connections between existing neurons (synaptogenesis), thereby potentially aiding in recovery from neurological damage and enhancing cognitive function.

Animal studies have provided substantial evidence for psilocybin's role in neuroplasticity. A landmark study in this domain, conducted by Dr. Juan R. Sanchez-Ramos and published in "Experimental Brain Research" in

2013, demonstrated that psilocybin could stimulate neurogenesis in the hippocampus of mice. The study found a significant increase in the number of new neurons in the hippocampal dentate gyrus, a region associated with memory and learning, after administering low doses of psilocybin.

Enhancement in Cognitive Flexibility and Learning

A study published in "Psychopharmacology" in 2020 explored the effects of psilocybin on cognitive flexibility. The research, involving a double-blind, placebo-controlled trial with participants who received either a single dose of psilocybin or a placebo, found that those who received psilocybin showed increased cognitive flexibility. This was measured using the Wisconsin Card Sorting Test (WCST), where psilocybin participants demonstrated an improved ability to switch between different categories, a direct indicator of cognitive flexibility. The study concluded that psilocybin could disrupt entrenched patterns of thought, potentially benefiting individuals suffering from conditions like depression and obsessive-compulsive disorder (OCD).

The burgeoning field of psychedelic research is gradually unraveling the intricate ways in which psilocybin may confer long-term neurological benefits. Far from being a fleeting journey, the effects of this compound may instigate a profound and enduring neurobiological renaissance, offering hope for therapeutic interventions in a variety of neurological and psychiatric conditions.

Addressing Concerns of Neurotoxicity

As the potential therapeutic benefits of psilocybin capture the scientific and medical communities' interest, it's crucial to address the elephant in the room: concerns about neurotoxicity. Current research is painting a reassuring picture, suggesting that psilocybin, when used responsibly, has a low potential for causing brain damage. Yet, the call for standardized dosing and longitudinal studies echoes the need for a cautious, evidence-based approach to unfolding the mysteries of this psychedelic compound.

Low Neurotoxicity Potential at Typical Doses

Psilocybin's neurotoxicity profile has been a subject of considerable interest, especially given the neurotoxic effects associated with other psychoactive substances such as MDMA. A comprehensive review published in the "Journal of Psychopharmacology" in 2018 assessed the safety and efficacy of psilocybin in controlled settings. The review examined various studies and clinical trials, finding no evidence of neurotoxic effects at typical doses used for therapeutic purposes. Notably, neuroimaging studies included in the review did not indicate any neurotoxic changes in brain structure or function following psilocybin administration.

Psilocybin's safety profile is further supported by data on its physiological toxicity and addiction potential. A comparative analysis in the journal "Lancet", ranking the harm of 20 drugs, placed psilocybin among the least harmful, significantly lower than alcohol and tobacco. Furthermore, psilocybin's potential for addiction is low, as evidenced by its mechanism of action on the serotonin 2A receptor, which does not typically engender the addictive behaviors associated with dopamine receptor activation.

Standardization of Dosage: Striking the Therapeutic Balance

Clinical trials for psilocybin therapy, including those sanctioned by the U.S. Food and Drug Administration (FDA) for treatment-resistant depression, are at the forefront of establishing safe and effective dosing parameters. For instance, a Phase 2 trial registered on ClinicalTrials.gov (NCT03775200) is examining the effects of varying doses of psilocybin (10, 25, and 25 mg/70 kg) on treatment-resistant depression. The study's design is crucial in determining the minimum effective dose that provides therapeutic benefits without undue side effects.

The variability in individual responses to psilocybin underscores the need for personalized dosing protocols. Ongoing research endeavors aim to identify biomarkers and psychological profiles that predict individual responses to psilocybin. This precision medicine approach is reflected in studies like the one published in the journal "Nature Medicine" in 2021, which utilized machine learning algorithms to predict individual responses to psychedelic-assisted therapy, emphasizing the potential for personalized treatment plans.

Longitudinal Studies: Charting the Long-Term Course

Institutions such as Johns Hopkins University are pioneering longitudinal research into the effects of psilocybin. For example, the Johns Hopkins Center for Psychedelic and Consciousness Research is conducting long-term studies to evaluate the enduring impacts of psilocybin-assisted therapy on psychological well being and cognitive function. These studies extend follow-up periods to several months or even years post-treatment to gather comprehensive data on the long-term efficacy and safety of psilocybin therapy.

Longitudinal studies are crucial for detecting any delayed or cumulative risks associated with psilocybin use. Ongoing research efforts, such as those documented in trial registries like ClinicalTrials.gov, include extended follow-up periods to monitor participants for potential adverse effects, changes in cognitive function, and signs of neurotoxicity that could manifest with repeated or long-term use. These studies are vital for constructing a complete risk-benefit profile of psilocybin, particularly for its potential role in chronic treatment regimens.

While the body of evidence tilts favorably towards a low risk of neurotoxicity from psilocybin, the scientific community remains vigilant. Standardized dosing and longitudinal studies are crucial for painting a comprehensive picture of psilocybin's impact on brain health. As research progresses, it's essential to maintain a balanced narrative that acknowledges both the potential benefits and the need for cautious, well-informed use of this intriguing psychedelic compound.

Conclusion

The dance between psilocybin and the brain is a complex tango marked by twists, turns, and unscripted moments of synergy. Within the dark labyrinths of the mind, psilocybin follows an intricate map of neurotransmitter pathways and circuits, binding with receptors and releasing a cascade of effects. What begins with the prosaic mechanics of blood flow and neural firing crescendos into a symphony of consciousness few can comprehend, yet many intuitively feel.

Modern imaging and research have illuminated snippets of this mystery, creating a lexicon to articulate the ineffable. Terms like "ego dissolution," "hyperconnectivity," and "neuroplasticity" now punctuate the literature. Yet phrases cannot encapsulate the totality of what unfolds within a human mind awakened to its furthest frontiers by psilocybin's psychic resonance.

The brain, ever illuminating while keeping its deepest secrets veiled, will continue to both guide and obscure the scientific mapping of psychedelia. But for those who have ventured inward and returned floored by what lies within, the relationship between consciousness and psilocybin transcends clinical semantics. It is primal, it is sacred, it is a dance as old as humanity itself.

CHAPTER 9: Beyond Psilocybin: Other Psychedelics

While psilocybin is prominent, it's one of many naturally occurring and synthetic psychedelic substances.

- Comparison with other psychedelics
- Synergy and combinations
- The broader psychedelic renaissance

The Psychedelic Tapestry: LSD, DMT, and Mescaline

The psychedelic landscape is rich and varied, with substances like LSD, DMT, and Mescaline painting unique strokes on the canvas of human consciousness. Each has its own history, cultural significance, and unique effects that have intrigued, mystified, and sometimes troubled societies throughout the ages. Here's an exploration of these three psychedelic substances, delving into their past, their profound effects on the human psyche, and the current landscape of research surrounding them.

LSD: The Synthesized Altered State

Albert Hofmann, working at Sandoz Laboratories, first synthesized LSD in 1938. Its psychedelic properties were accidentally discovered on April 19, 1943, a day now known as "Bicycle Day," when Hofmann ingested a small amount (250 micrograms) and experienced profound changes in perception during his ride home.

LSD is a potent serotonin agonist, primarily affecting the 5-HT2A receptor, which is thought to play a key role in its psychedelic effects. These effects include profound alterations in sensory perception, mood, and cognition. Hallucinations can be both visual and auditory, and users often report a dissolution of ego or sense of self.

Recent research has revitalized interest in LSD's therapeutic potential. A study published in the "Journal of Psychopharmacology" in 2016 investigated the impact of LSD on end-of-life anxiety in patients with life-threatening diseases. The double-blind, placebo-controlled study found significant reductions in anxiety following two LSD-assisted psychotherapy sessions. The results indicated a sustained benefit, with anxiety reductions maintained at a 12-month follow-up.

A 2021 study in "Nature Medicine" advanced our understanding of LSD's therapeutic effects. In this randomized, double-blind, placebo-controlled phase 2 trial involving 40 participants, LSD-assisted therapy demonstrated a significant reduction in anxiety among patients with life-threatening diseases. Notably, the anxiolytic effects of a single LSD session were evident up to two weeks after treatment, underscoring its potential as a lasting therapeutic intervention.

Albert Hofmann - "Bicycle Day"

Albert Hofmann, a Swiss chemist, synthesized lysergic acid diethylamide, more commonly known as LSD, for the first time on November 16, 1938, while working at Sandoz Laboratories (now a part of Novartis) in Basel, Switzerland. Hofmann was not initially searching for a psychedelic substance; his primary goal was to create a respiratory and circulatory stimulant as part of a program to purify and synthesize active constituents of medicinal plants. LSD was the 25th compound in a series of derivatives synthesized from ergot alkaloids that were derived from ergot, a fungus that grows on rye and other grains.

However, the initial tests on animals did not yield the expected results, and the substance didn't show any particularly useful medical properties, so the research on LSD was shelved.

Five years later, on April 16, 1943, Hofmann decided to revisit the substance. He accidentally absorbed a small amount through his fingertips and reported strange sensations, including restlessness and dizziness, prompting him to further explore its effects. Three days later, on April 19, 1943, Hofmann intentionally ingested 250 micrograms of LSD, which he believed to be a threshold dose (it is, in fact, quite a robust dose by modern standards). The effects were dramatic and unlike anything he had ever experienced.

Feeling overwhelmed by the substance's powerful effects, Hofmann decided to return home from the laboratory. Because of wartime restrictions and his impaired state, he made the journey by bicycle, accompanied by his laboratory assistant. During the ride, he experienced intense changes in perception, including visual distortions, an altered sense of time and space, and vivid colorations.

Upon reaching home, Hofmann's condition did not improve. Fearing he had poisoned himself, he called for a doctor. Despite his altered state, a subsequent examination found him to be in good physical health, although he was in a highly disturbed psychological state. This experience marked the world's first acid trip, and April 19 has been celebrated since as "Bicycle Day" in commemoration of this unprecedented and historic event.

The discovery of LSD's psychoactive properties had a profound impact on Hofmann, who later described LSD as a "sacred drug" and was known to have used it a number of times throughout his life. He recognized its potential for psychotherapeutic uses and also advocated for its responsible use in exploring the human mind.

DMT: The Spirit Molecule

DMT has been used for centuries in South American shamanic rituals, most notably in the form of Ayahuasca. Ayahuasca is a brew made from the Banisteriopsis caapi vine and DMT-containing plants, used traditionally for spiritual and healing purposes.

DMT is renowned for its rapid onset (often within seconds when smoked or vaporized) and intense effects, which can include the sensation of transcending one's body, encountering entities, and experiencing other realities. The "breakthrough" experience is often described as life-changing by users.

A study published in "Frontiers in Psychology" in 2016 explored the potential therapeutic effects of Ayahuasca. The research focused on its impact on mental health, finding significant reductions in depression and anxiety scores among participants. The study also noted improvements in mindfulness and overall well-being.

Further elucidating DMT's mechanism of action, a 2019 study in "Psychological Medicine" revealed Ayahuasca's influence on neuroplasticity. Researchers observed a significant increase in brain-derived neurotrophic factor (BDNF) levels following a single Ayahuasca session, suggesting a biological basis for the compound's reported therapeutic effects, particularly in the realms of mental health and cognitive function.

Mescaline: The Natural Psychedelic

Mescaline has been used for at least 5,700 years by indigenous peoples in what is now Mexico and the Southwestern United States. The Peyote cactus, which contains mescaline, is considered sacred in many Native American cultures and is central to the religious rituals of the Native American Church.

Mescaline's effects are often described as being more "earthly" and less overwhelming than those of LSD or DMT. Users report vivid colors, geometric patterns, and a profound sense of connection to nature and the universe.

Research into mescaline's therapeutic potential is less advanced than that of LSD or psilocybin. However, organizations like MAPS are beginning to investigate its potential in clinical settings. An observational study published by MAPS in 2013 examined the effects of Peyote on mental health among members of the Native American Church. The study found no evidence of psychological or cognitive deficits among the participants, suggesting a safety profile conducive to further research.

In 2020, "Drugs: Education, Prevention and Policy" published findings that shed light on mescaline's potential mental health benefits. Survey data from Native Americans who partook in ceremonial Peyote use revealed an association with lower levels of psychological distress, reinforcing the notion that mescaline's historical usage in spiritual contexts may harbor contemporary therapeutic applications.

LSD, DMT, and Mescaline are potent psychoactive substances, each with unique historical, cultural, and pharmacological profiles. Current research is shedding new light on their therapeutic potential, particularly in the treatment of mental health conditions.

The Psychedelic Spectrum: LSD, DMT, and Mescaline

The psychedelic realm is a mosaic of experiences characterized by substances that, while sharing common mechanisms of action, manifest unique psychological and physiological effects. LSD, DMT, and Mescaline are three such substances, each providing a distinct lens through which the human consciousness can be examined and expanded.

Common Mechanisms of Action

LSD, DMT, and Mescaline exert their psychedelic effects primarily through the serotonergic system by acting as agonists at the serotonin 5-HT2A receptors. This receptor subtype is widely distributed in the brain, particularly in regions involved in cognition and perception, such as the prefrontal cortex.

Emerging research continues to uncover the nuances of how psychedelics interact with the serotonergic system. A study published in "Nature" in 2020 provided deeper insights into the molecular dynamics of LSD's interaction with the 5-HT2A receptor. Using cryo-electron microscopy, researchers visualized the exact conformation of LSD bound to the receptor, revealing why its effects last unusually long. The LSD molecule gets trapped within the receptor by a lid-like domain, explaining its prolonged binding and the extended duration of its psychedelic effects.

A study published in the journal Cell Reports in 2018 provides evidence for the role of psychedelics in promoting neural plasticity. The study showed that psychedelics, including LSD and DMT, promote neuritogenesis, spinogenesis, and synaptogenesis in vitro and in vivo. This means they can enhance the structural and functional rewiring of brain cells, which is critical in learning and memory and potentially in the repair and recovery of brain function in psychiatric diseases.

In addition to promoting neuroplasticity, recent studies suggest psychedelics might also facilitate 'neural harmony,' enhancing brain connectivity. A research article published in "Scientific Reports" in 2020 used functional magnetic resonance imaging (fMRI) to show that LSD induces a more unified brain state. This state, characterized by increased global connectivity and decreased modular brain structure, may underlie the unique conscious experiences induced by LSD, such as ego-dissolution and altered perception.

Unique Psychological and Physiological Effects

LSD: Users often report profound shifts in consciousness with LSD, including synesthesia (mixing of the senses, such as "seeing" sounds), altered perception of time, and ego dissolution. On a physiological level, LSD can cause pupil dilation, increased body temperature, heart rate, and blood pressure. The effects can last up to 12 hours due to its strong binding affinity and slow dissociation from the 5-HT2A receptor.

DMT: DMT is unique due to its rapid onset and intense psychedelic experience, often characterized by complex visual hallucinations and encounters with entity-like figures. The intensity is likely due to its efficient crossing of the blood-brain barrier and its strong affinity for the 5-HT2A receptor. Physiologically, DMT can induce a rapid increase in heart rate and blood pressure. The smoked or vaporized form of DMT produces a short-acting effect, typically lasting 15-60 minutes.

Mescaline: Mescaline leads to a less intense but longer-lasting psychedelic experience compared to DMT, often described as more empathogenic and introspective. Users report a heightened sense of clarity, euphoria, and a profound connection with nature. Physiological effects include pupil dilation, increased heart rate, and nausea. The duration of mescaline's effects, when ingested orally, can last between 10 to 12 hours.\

Variations in Duration and Intensity

LSD and mescaline share a similar duration profile, with effects lasting up to 10-12 hours. This is partly due to their metabolic pathways and slow dissociation from their target receptors. DMT, on the other hand, especially when smoked or vaporized, has a brief duration of effect, generally 15-60 minutes, due to its rapid metabolism by monoamine oxidase enzymes.

DMT stands out for its sudden and profound intensity, often catapulting users into a completely different perceptual dimension within moments. LSD can also produce intense experiences, but these unfold more gradually and linger for a longer duration. Mescaline, while still producing profound psychedelic effects, is often described as having a more gentle onset and a less overwhelming intensity than LSD or DMT.

The route of administration influences the onset, intensity, and duration of the psychedelic experience. LSD is typically taken orally, often via blotter paper, which leads to a gradual onset of effects. DMT, when smoked or vaporized, has an almost immediate onset due to its rapid absorption into the bloodstream and subsequent crossing of the blood-brain barrier. Mescaline, usually consumed orally from cacti preparations like Peyote or San Pedro, has a slower onset and longer duration, akin to LSD.

Novel formulations of psychedelic compounds are expanding the possibilities for their route of administration. A study from "European Neuropsychopharmacology" in 2021 investigated the pharmacokinetics of intranasal DMT. The results showed that intranasal administration led to a rapid onset of effects akin to smoking or vaporization but with a potentially more controlled and titratable administration method. This could have significant implications for the therapeutic use of DMT, allowing for a fast-acting yet manageable approach.

Each of these psychedelics presents a unique profile in terms of its mechanisms of action, psychological and physiological effects, and variations in duration and intensity. Understanding these differences is crucial for both therapeutic applications and harm-reduction practices in recreational settings.

While LSD, DMT, and Mescaline share common serotonergic mechanisms, their psychological and physiological effects, as well as their durations and intensities, vary greatly. These differences underscore the diversity within the psychedelic experience and highlight the importance of context, setting, and individual factors in shaping these profound encounters with altered states of consciousness.

Synergy and Combinations

In the vast landscape of psychedelic experiences, users often experiment with combinations of substances, seeking unique synergies and altered states of consciousness. Popular combinations have gained their own vernacular among users, such as "candy-flipping" and "hippie-flipping." While anecdotal reports abound, scientific investigation into these combinations is limited, leaving much to be understood about their potential effects and risks.

Definitions of Psychedelic Combinations

Candy-flipping

Candy-flipping combines LSD, a potent psychedelic known for its profound changes in thought patterns and sensory perception, with MDMA, a substance with strong empathogenic and euphoric effects. Users of this combination report experiences of heightened emotional insight and visual enhancement, often describing it as a harmonious blend of the introspective nature of LSD with the warmth and sociability brought on by MDMA. This combination is usually timed so that the peak effects of both substances align, often involving taking MDMA 3-4 hours after ingesting LSD.

While the subjective experiences of candy-flipping are widely discussed in anecdotal reports, clinical research into the combined effects of LSD and MDMA remains scarce. However, harm reduction organizations like DanceSafe and the Multidisciplinary Association for Psychedelic Studies (MAPS) provide educational resources based on user experiences and medical expertise. These resources emphasize the importance of dose management, setting, and hydration when engaging in such practices.

Hippie-flipping

Hippie-flipping, or flower-flipping, involves the combination of psilocybin mushrooms, which contain the psychedelic compound psilocybin, with MDMA. Psilocybin mushrooms can induce profound changes in perception, emotion, and a sense of spiritual connectedness. When combined with MDMA, users report a smoothing of the intense introspection and occasional emotional turbulence associated with mushrooms, leading to a more euphoric and less challenging experience. This combination also tends to be timed, with MDMA often taken after the peak effects of the mushrooms begin to manifest.

Similar to candy-flipping, empirical research on hippie-flipping is limited. However, individual components of the experience, such as the effects of psilocybin and MDMA, have been the subject of clinical studies. For instance, MDMA-assisted psychotherapy for PTSD is currently in phase 3 clinical trials conducted by MAPS, while psilocybin has been granted Breakthrough Therapy designation by the FDA for depression. These studies provide a scientific basis for understanding the individual effects of these substances, although their combined effects remain underexplored.

Jedi-flipping

Jedi-flipping is the simultaneous use of three psychoactive substances: LSD, MDMA, and psilocybin mushrooms. This combination is considered highly intense and complex, given the potent and diverse effects of each substance. Users report experiences that can be deeply euphoric, insightful, and visually spectacular but also warn of the potential for overwhelming intensity and challenging psychological experiences. Due to the powerful and synergistic nature of this combination, it is considered highly unpredictable and carries significant risks.

Potential Effects and Risks

The synergistic effects of these combinations can lead to experiences that are qualitatively different from those produced by any of the substances alone. Users report enhanced sensory perception, with visual and auditory inputs becoming more vivid and emotionally impactful. Emotional breakthroughs, including profound feelings of love, empathy, and interconnectedness, are commonly reported. However, the unpredictability of these combinations can also lead to unexpectedly intense and potentially overwhelming experiences.

Combining psychoactive substances increases the risk of adverse effects. Serotonin syndrome, characterized by symptoms such as confusion, rapid heart rate, and high blood pressure, can occur due to the combined serotonergic effects of these substances. Cardiovascular strain, dehydration, and hyperthermia are also concerns, particularly in settings such as music festivals where users may be dancing for extended periods without adequate hydration.

The interactions between LSD, MDMA, and psilocybin mushrooms can vary widely among individuals. Factors such as individual physiology, mental state, setting, dosage, and the purity of the substances can significantly influence the experience. This unpredictability underscores the inherent risks associated with these combinations, as users may have difficulty anticipating the intensity and nature of the effects.

Anecdotal and Scientific Evidence

Online forums, such as those found on Erowid, Reddit, and Bluelight, contain numerous anecdotal reports of these combinations. These accounts often emphasize the profound and transformative nature of the experiences, highlighting moments of deep emotional catharsis and sensory beauty. However, negative experiences, including panic attacks, confusion, and disorientation, are also documented, illustrating the potential risks and challenges.

Scientific research on the combinations of LSD, MDMA, and psilocybin mushrooms is limited due to legal and ethical constraints. However, a study published in "Drug and Alcohol Dependence" explored the subjective effects of combining MDMA with LSD. The study found that the combination led to increased cardiovascular effects and distinctive changes in subjective experience compared to either drug alone. The authors suggested potential therapeutic applications but cautioned about the increased physiological strain associated with the combination. This research is an exception rather than the norm, as most of the knowledge about these combinations comes from anecdotal reports and harm reduction literature.

While psychedelic combinations like candy-flipping and hippie-flipping are discussed anecdotally within user communities, there is a significant gap in scientific understanding. These practices entail complex interactions that can amplify both the positive and negative aspects of the psychedelic experience. As such, individuals considering such combinations should approach them with caution, awareness of the potential risks, and ideally, under the guidance of a knowledgeable and experienced practitioner.

Safety Concerns and Enhancing Experiences

Exploring the realms of psychedelic experiences can be transformative, yet it comes with inherent risks. Enhancing safety and ensuring positive outcomes involves meticulous preparation and informed strategies.

Risk Mitigation Strategies

In the realm of psychedelics, the purity and authenticity of a substance are paramount for safety. Substance testing, often facilitated by reagent testing kits, involves chemical reactions that indicate the presence of specific compounds. For instance, the Marquis reagent turns purple in the presence of MDMA. Organizations like DanceSafe and Bunk Police have popularized the use of such kits at festivals and events. These organizations also offer online guides for interpreting results, though it's worth noting that reagent tests can indicate the presence of a substance but not its purity or concentration.

Access to accurate, unbiased information is critical for harm reduction in psychedelic use. Erowid is a well-known online resource that houses a vast repository of information, including user experiences, dosage guidelines, and legal status for a myriad of substances. Another resource, The Third Wave, focuses on providing educational content aimed at changing the cultural conversation around psychedelics and promoting safe and responsible use. These platforms operate on the principle that informed users are better equipped to make safer choices.

In clinical research and therapeutic settings, the presence of medical professionals during psychedelic sessions can significantly enhance safety. This is particularly vital for individuals with pre-existing health conditions that could be exacerbated by psychedelic use. Clinical trials investigating the therapeutic potential of psychedelics often include medical supervision as a standard protocol. For example, in psilocybin trials conducted at Johns Hopkins University, participants are monitored by medical professionals in a controlled setting to promptly address any adverse reactions.

The Role of Integration and Harm Reduction

Integration is the process by which the insights and revelations from a psychedelic experience are incorporated into one's life. This can involve therapeutic sessions with professionals trained in psychedelic integration, such as those affiliated with MAPS (Multidisciplinary Association for Psychedelic Studies).

Harm reduction is a public health philosophy that seeks to reduce the negative consequences associated with drug use without necessarily requiring cessation of drug use. This approach includes providing factual information, advocating for policies that prioritize health, and offering supportive services. The Zendo Project is an initiative that embodies these principles, providing a safe space and trained volunteers to assist individuals undergoing challenging psychedelic experiences at events. By focusing on support rather than punishment, harm reduction initiatives aim to promote safety, dignity, and well-being.

While the potential of psychedelics for personal growth and healing is significant, it is paralleled by the need for conscientious risk mitigation, an understanding of 'set and setting,' and dedicated integration and harm reduction efforts. Through these measures, individuals can enhance the safety and efficacy of their psychedelic experiences, aligning them more closely with their intentions and well-being.

Conclusion

The domain of psychedelics is far more than the singular note of psilocybin. It is a symphony of compounds, each adding distinct melodies and rhythms to the score of human consciousness. The flute-like visionarium of DMT, the electric guitar wail of LSD, and the subtle sitar tones of mescaline collectively beckon us into a deeper exploration of mind, perspective, and reality itself.

While bound by a common thread of psychoactivity, differences in intensity, duration, and effect ensure that no two journeys are identical. Each experience reveals its own treasures and challenges to integrate. Used judiciously, combinations may harmonize complimentary qualities, yet unpredictability persists.

As research expands, the possibilities and applications of psychedelics continue to multiply through a kaleidoscopic lens, revealing ever-new facets of healing, creativity, and imagination. Yet their timeless call to humanity persists—to move beyond the manacles of perception and into the unbounded vistas that exist within. Echoing this invitation, psilocybin and its molecular cousins remind us why, after all this time, the irresistible temptation to explore inner space endures.

CHAPTER 10: The Psilocybin Debate in Scientific Circles

"Psilocybin mushrooms could be the next medical marijuana in terms of an unstoppable social movement that addresses health conditions."

Paul Stamets, Mycologist

- Delve into safety, ethical, and societal issues raised
- Explore the challenges in legal and policy landscapes
- Examine emerging research balancing risks and rewards

In the realm of scientific research, few subjects have sparked as much debate as psilocybin, a naturally occurring psychedelic compound. This debate is marked by a complex interplay of perspectives, ranging from enthusiastic support based on its therapeutic potential to serious concerns about its safety and societal impact. By examining safety issues, methodological critiques, and ethical and societal implications, we offer a comprehensive overview of the critical perspective on psilocybin research.

Safety Concerns

The use of psilocybin, though showing promising therapeutic benefits, comes with its set of safety concerns. These concerns span psychological risks, potential physical health impacts, and the dangers associated with uncontrolled use.

Psychological Risks

Psilocybin can trigger intense psychological reactions, particularly in individuals predisposed to mental health disorders. The phenomenon of "bad trips" is characterized by severe anxiety, paranoia, and frightening hallucinations. A study in the "Journal of Psychopharmacology" reported that some individuals experienced persisting adverse effects, such as anxiety and disorientation, after using psilocybin.

The long-term psychological impact is a growing area of concern. For some individuals, psilocybin use has been linked to persistent changes in perception and mood, known as Hallucinogen Persisting Perception Disorder (HPPD). While rare, this condition can significantly affect one's quality of life.

There is evidence suggesting that psilocybin may precipitate the onset of psychiatric conditions like schizophrenia in individuals who are genetically predisposed. Careful screening for family history of mental health disorders is a critical step in mitigating this risk in clinical settings.

Physical Health Risks

Psilocybin can induce changes in heart rate and blood pressure, posing risks to individuals with cardiovascular conditions. A study in "The American Journal of Cardiology" highlighted the need for caution in individuals with a history of heart disease when considering psilocybin therapy.

Psilocybin can interact with other drugs, particularly those affecting the serotonin system, such as SSRIs or MAOIs. This can lead to adverse reactions, emphasizing the need for careful medical oversight and a detailed understanding of a patient's medication regimen.

In non-clinical settings, the lack of control over dosage and purity can lead to physical risks. Accidental ingestion of toxic varieties of mushrooms, mistaking them for psilocybin-containing ones, is a documented hazard.

Uncontrolled Use and Settings

The use of psilocybin in unregulated environments can lead to risky behaviors due to impaired judgment and altered perception. There are cases of accidents and injuries reported during unsupervised psychedelic experiences.

The lack of standardization in the potency and purity of psilocybin mushrooms available recreationally adds to the risk profile. Variations in psilocybin content can lead to unpredictable and potentially dangerous experiences.

The importance of controlled settings for psilocybin use is underscored by research emphasizing the role of "set and setting" in shaping the psychedelic experience. In clinical trials, protocols are designed to ensure a safe and supportive environment, significantly reducing the risks associated with psilocybin use.

Small Sample Sizes

Many psilocybin studies involve a limited number of participants, raising concerns about the statistical power and generalizability of the findings. A review article in the American Journal of Psychiatry pointed out that while smaller studies have shown positive results, they may not accurately represent the broader population.

Early-phase clinical trials, such as those conducted by Johns Hopkins University and New York University, have typically involved fewer than 100 participants. Although these studies have been pivotal in demonstrating the potential of psilocybin, their small size limits the ability to detect rare side effects or to understand the variability in individual responses.

Future research should aim for larger, more diverse participant pools. Collaborative multi-center trials could help in recruiting a sufficient number of participants to ensure that findings are robust and widely applicable.

Placebo Challenges

The unique and often profound effects of psilocybin make it difficult to employ effective placebo controls. Participants can usually discern whether they have received the active compound or a placebo, which can influence their expectations and experiences during the trial.

A critique in Neuropsychopharmacology highlighted the difficulty of maintaining blinding in psychedelic research. In trials where participants easily identify the active drug, placebo effects can be significantly altered, impacting the study's validity.

Researchers are exploring novel methods to address this issue, such as using active placebos that mimic some effects of psilocybin or employing balanced crossover designs where all participants eventually receive psilocybin.

Long-term Effects Unclear

There is a lack of long-term data on the effects of psilocybin. Critics argue that understanding the full scope of potential risks, especially with repeated use, requires long-term observational studies.

Most psilocybin studies have focused on immediate and short-term effects, often within a few months post-treatment. This leaves a gap in knowledge regarding the long-term safety profile of psilocybin, especially concerning cognitive, psychological, and physiological outcomes.

Longitudinal studies tracking individuals for several years post-psilocybin use are necessary. These studies should monitor for potential negative outcomes, such as changes in cognitive function, the emergence of psychiatric symptoms, or the development of substance use disorders.

Recreational vs. Therapeutic Use

Distinguishing between recreational and therapeutic use of psilocybin is challenging. While its therapeutic potential is being increasingly recognized, there is a concern that promoting its benefits might inadvertently encourage recreational use, which can be risky without proper guidance and setting.

Psilocybin has been used recreationally since the 1960s, often associated with the counterculture movement. While some users report profound, life-changing experiences, others have faced psychological distress and legal consequences.

Public education campaigns and clear guidelines are essential to inform people about the safe, responsible use of psilocybin. Professional medical oversight for therapeutic use is crucial to distinguish it from recreational use. For example, the Beckley Foundation advocates for evidence-based drug policies that separate therapeutic use from recreational abuse.

Commodification and Cultural Appropriation

The increasing interest of pharmaceutical companies in psilocybin raises questions about the commodification of a substance traditionally used in indigenous rituals and spiritual practices. This commercialization could potentially strip these practices of their cultural significance.

Indigenous groups have used psilocybin for centuries in sacred rituals. The concern is that commercialization could lead to cultural appropriation, neglecting the sacred context in which these substances are traditionally used.

Ensuring that indigenous communities are involved in and benefit from the commercialization of psilocybin is crucial. Initiatives like the North Star Project are working towards ethical guidelines to prevent exploitation and ensure that indigenous knowledge is respected and preserved.

Regulatory and Legal Challenges

The legal status of psilocybin is evolving, with cities like Denver and Oakland decriminalizing its use and Oregon legalizing it for therapeutic use.

The integration of psilocybin into healthcare systems poses significant regulatory challenges. Policymakers must balance the potential therapeutic benefits with concerns about safety, abuse, and public health implications.

As outlined in publications like the "Harvard Law Review", there are ongoing debates about the ethical implications of legal changes. Issues include ensuring access for therapeutic purposes while preventing misuse, addressing the stigma associated with psychedelic use, and the potential impact on criminal justice systems.

Future Directions and Unanswered Questions

The exploration of psilocybin, a compound with both controversial history and promising therapeutic potential, stands at a crossroads. As research delves deeper into its effects and applications, the future trajectory of psilocybin is shaped not only by scientific findings but also by societal attitudes and regulatory frameworks.

Need for Rigorous Clinical Trials

Comprehensive clinical trials are essential to validate the safety and effectiveness of psilocybin. These studies need to be large-scale and methodologically sound to produce reliable data.

Johns Hopkins University and other institutions are conducting extensive research into psilocybin's potential for treating various mental health disorders. For instance, their trials on psilocybin for depression and PTSD aim to understand dosing, efficacy, and potential risks.

These trials adhere to regulatory standards like those set by the FDA, ensuring that the research is ethical scientifically valid, and that participant safety is prioritized. This includes rigorous participant screening, informed consent processes, and close monitoring of participants throughout the study.

Standardized Dosing Protocols

Establishing standardized dosing protocols for psilocybin is complex due to individual variations in response. Factors like body weight, metabolic rate, and personal sensitivity to the substance can significantly impact the experience.

Studies in "Psychopharmacology" have begun to analyze how different doses affect individuals, aiming to develop a more standardized approach. For example, researchers are exploring whether fixed doses or weight-based dosing provide more consistent therapeutic outcomes.

Standardized dosing is crucial for both therapeutic applications and minimizing the risk of adverse effects. This will also aid in the development of guidelines for practitioners who may administer psilocybin in clinical settings.

Development of Safe Administration Protocols

The creation of protocols for the safe administration of psilocybin is essential, especially in therapeutic contexts. This includes the physical setting, the presence of trained professionals, and guidelines for managing potential adverse reactions.

Professionals overseeing psilocybin sessions require specialized training. This includes understanding the pharmacology of psilocybin, managing the psychological aspects of psychedelic experiences, and emergency procedures for adverse events.

Protocols for adverse reactions are a critical component. This could involve immediate psychological support, medical intervention, and follow-up care. Studies have shown that with proper support, most adverse reactions can be effectively managed, minimizing long-term negative effects.

Influence of Media and Cultural Narratives

The portrayal of psilocybin in various media forms, including documentaries, news articles, and social media, plays a crucial role in shaping public opinion. Positive coverage in reputable media outlets can enhance public understanding and acceptance.

Publications like "The New York Times" have featured articles that present psilocybin research in a positive light, focusing on its potential therapeutic benefits. Similarly, documentaries such as "Fantastic Fungi" have educated audiences about the science and potential of psilocybin, contributing to a shift in public perception.

As media narratives evolve, they reflect and contribute to broader cultural shifts. The change from viewing psychedelics solely as recreational drugs to potential therapeutic agents mirrors this evolving narrative.

Impact on Policy and Research Funding

Public opinion can exert a significant influence on policy decisions regarding psilocybin research and legalization. A positive shift in perception can lead to progressive policies, as seen with the decriminalization movements in certain U.S. cities.

Public support often translates into increased funding opportunities for psychedelic research. For instance, the recent growth in psilocybin research can be partially attributed to the changing public opinion, which has encouraged private and public entities to invest in this field.

The comparison with cannabis is instructive; as public opinion shifted towards recognizing its medical benefits, there was a corresponding increase in research funding and legislative changes.

Education and Advocacy

Organizations like MAPS play a vital role in educating the public, advocating for policy change, and funding clinical trials. Their efforts in disseminating accurate information help counteract misinformation and stigma.

These organizations engage in various outreach activities, including public lectures, informational websites, and participation in scientific conferences, to spread awareness about the therapeutic potentials and safety profiles of psychedelics like psilocybin.

Navigating Stigmas and Misconceptions

Addressing Stigmas: Overcoming the longstanding stigmas associated with psilocybin, which stem from its history as an illicit substance, is crucial. Efforts to reframe psilocybin as a potential therapeutic agent involve highlighting rigorous scientific research and clinical trials.

Clear communication about the differences between controlled therapeutic use and recreational misuse is essential. Public education campaigns can clarify misconceptions, emphasizing the controlled, safe, and potentially beneficial use of psilocybin in therapeutic settings.

Public perception plays a critical role in shaping the future of psilocybin as a therapeutic agent. Through informed media portrayals, policy advocacy, education, and addressing misconceptions, the path toward wider acceptance and integration of psilocybin in medicine can be paved. Continued efforts in these areas are crucial to fostering an environment where the potential benefits of psilocybin can be fully explored and utilized.

Conclusion

The budding promise of psilocybin is not without its share of questions, concerns and controversies within the scientific community. Optimism must be tempered with rigor when evaluating a substance that elicits such profound alterations of consciousness. Reconciling therapeutic potential with societal risks requires ethical frameworks and thoughtful policies.

Yet the psychedelic experience, for all its mystery, bows to the tested tools of science. Researchers continue to move these discussions from polemics to empirics, gathering data, refining methodologies, and mapping uncharted neurological terrain. The gaps in current understanding summon a spirit of open yet critical inquiry from all who engage in this dialogue.

As the rhapsody of discovery and debate surrounding psilocybin continues, the course ahead will be shaped not just by research but by cultural narratives, political winds, and a reimagining of society's relationship with psychedelic substances. With insights from ancient healing traditions intersecting with modern science, there is hope that the eventual synthesis will be greater than the sum of its parts. Guided thus, psilocybin's promise may be fulfilled, conferred through the rigorous work of dedicated scientists, therapists, advocates and an open-minded public willing to put aside old prejudices.

CHAPTER 11: Interview with Traditional Healer Nayeli

In a world increasingly fascinated by the therapeutic potentials of psychedelics, traditional practices involving these substances offer invaluable insights. Psilocybin mushrooms, in particular, have been a subject of both scientific interest and cultural intrigue. To delve deeper into the rich tapestry of traditional knowledge surrounding these mystical fungi, we turn to the indigenous communities that have revered and utilized them for centuries.

In this exclusive interview, we sit down with Nayeli, a traditional healer from the Mazatec region of Mexico, renowned for its long-standing relationship with psilocybin mushrooms. Nayeli, a name that resonates with love in the Zapotec language, comes from a lineage of curanderos (healers) and has dedicated her life to the spiritual and healing practices rooted in her culture.

Our conversation explores the sacredness of psilocybin in traditional healing ceremonies, the intricate preparations involved, and the profound impact these experiences have on individuals. Nayeli sheds light on the misconceptions surrounding the use of these mushrooms and emphasizes their role as a bridge to deeper self-awareness and spiritual enlightenment, far from their often misunderstood recreational use.

This interview aims to bridge the gap between ancient wisdom and modern curiosity, offering a rare glimpse into the mystical world of psilocybin as seen through the eyes of a traditional Mazatec healer. We embark on this enlightening journey, uncovering the nuances of a practice deeply embedded in respect, spirituality, and the healing power of nature.

Isabella Rodriguez: Today, we're speaking with Nayeli, a respected traditional healer from the Mazatec region of Mexico. Nayeli, thank you for joining us. Could you start by telling us about your background as a healer?

Nayeli: Thank you for having me. Yes, I come from a lineage rich in healing traditions deeply rooted in the Mazatec culture. Healing, for us, is more than just a practice; it's a way of life, a communion with the natural world. My ancestors were curanderos, known for their profound understanding of medicinal plants and spiritual rituals. From a young age, I was immersed in this world, learning to understand the language of plants and the subtleties of energy that flow through all living things.

Isabella Rodriguez: Psilocybe mushrooms are known for their psychoactive properties. How do you view these mushrooms in your healing practices?

Nayeli: In our tradition, psilocybe mushrooms are revered as sacred beings, not merely as substances. They are seen as keys that unlock the deeper chambers of the human psyche, allowing us to converse with the unseen realms. We believe that these mushrooms have spirits, and when we consume them, it's an act of entering a sacred dialogue.

In our healing ceremonies, these mushrooms are used as tools for deep introspection and spiritual renewal. They help in cleansing the soul and bringing to light the inner conflicts and traumas that often lie buried in the subconscious. This process, though deeply healing, is also demanding and requires guidance. It's akin to navigating a vast ocean - the mushrooms are the vessel, but one still needs a skilled navigator to reach the destination safely.

Their use is not recreational but a sacrament, a serious endeavor undertaken in a ceremonial context. It's about setting intentions and seeking insights, and often, it's a pathway to healing deep-rooted emotional and psychological wounds. The experience can be transformative, allowing individuals to confront and integrate aspects of themselves that they've been unaware of or avoided.

In essence, these mushrooms act as mirrors, reflecting back to us our deepest fears, joys, and the untapped potential that lies within. They remind us of our interconnectedness with nature and the universe, often leading to profound feelings of oneness and empathy. This understanding is crucial for healing not just the individual but also the community as a whole.

Isabella Rodriguez: How do you prepare for a healing ceremony involving these mushrooms?

Nayeli: The preparation for a psilocybin ceremony is a careful and reverent process. Firstly, we approach the gathering of the mushrooms with utmost respect. Traditionally, this is done at dawn, when the world is still and nature's energy is most potent. The mushrooms are not merely picked; they are received with gratitude, often accompanied by a small offering or prayer to the earth. This practice stems from our belief that everything in nature is alive and sacred.

From a spiritual perspective, both the healer and the participant engage in various purifying practices. This could include fasting for at least a day before the ceremony to cleanse the body. We also encourage participants to engage in introspective practices like meditation and prayer, which help in centering their minds and setting intentions. This spiritual groundwork is vital as it helps in creating a receptive state of mind, crucial for the deep, introspective journey that follows.

Isabella Rodriguez: Can you walk us through what happens during a typical ceremony?

Nayeli: Certainly. Our ceremonies are deeply rooted in tradition and are typically held at night, symbolizing a journey from darkness to light, from unconsciousness to consciousness. The setting is quiet and sacred, often adorned with elements from nature and symbolic artifacts. This environment is crucial as it fosters a sense of safety and sanctity.

Once everyone is settled, the ceremony begins with prayers and offerings, invoking spiritual guidance and protection. The mushrooms are then distributed, and each participant consumes them, usually in silence, reflecting on their intentions. The onset of the mushrooms' effects can vary, but as the healer, I remain attentive to the needs of each individual.

As the journey progresses, I use chants, music, and sometimes rhythmic drumming to guide and support the experience. These sounds are not random; they are integral to our tradition and believed to help in navigating the psychedelic experience. The chants often passed down through generations, are more than just words; they are vibrations that resonate with the psyche, aiding in the healing process.

During the peak of the experience, participants might encounter a range of emotions and visions. My role is to provide a reassuring presence, helping them navigate through difficult or intense moments. This might involve offering words of comfort, holding space, or sometimes just being a silent, supportive presence.

As the effects of the mushrooms begin to wane, we gradually bring the ceremony to a close, often with a sharing circle where participants can express their experiences and insights. This sharing is a vital part of integration, as it allows individuals to process and make sense of their journey.

The entire experience is a blend of the mystical and the therapeutic, deeply personal, yet connected to the collective consciousness of our culture. It's a journey of healing, discovery, and, often, profound transformation.

Isabella Rodriguez: What do participants typically seek from these experiences?

Nayeli: The reasons individuals come to these ceremonies are as diverse as the people themselves. However, there are common themes. Many participants seek healing from deep-seated emotional wounds or traumas that have impacted their lives. They often carry burdens that conventional therapies have not fully addressed, and they look to mushrooms for a different kind of healing.

Others come in search of guidance for significant life decisions or transitions. They may feel at a crossroads, uncertain about their path, and seek clarity and direction. The psilocybin experience, in its ability to break down barriers of the ego, can offer profound insights and reveal new perspectives.

Then, there are those who seek a deeper connection with the spiritual aspect of their existence. They wish to delve into the mystical, to feel a sense of oneness with the universe, or to explore the deeper layers of their consciousness.

What's remarkable about these mushrooms is their ability to reveal truths that are hidden deep within one's psyche. They act as a mirror, reflecting back aspects of the self that might be ignored or suppressed. This can be a challenging process, but it is often where the greatest healing and understanding occur.

Isabella Rodriguez: Are there any misconceptions about psilocybin mushrooms that you'd like to address?

Nayeli: Certainly. One major misconception is viewing these mushrooms merely as recreational "drugs" used for escapism or entertainment. In our tradition, they are sacred medicine, approached with great reverence and respect. Their purpose is not to escape reality but to confront it more deeply. The experiences they facilitate are often intense and introspective, requiring a level of readiness and maturity from the participants.

Another misconception is the belief that these mushrooms can be harmful or lead to addiction. While they are powerful and must be approached with caution and respect, they are not addictive in the way many substances are. In fact, they can be tools for liberation from other addictive behaviors and mindsets.

It's also important to dispel the fear that surrounds their use. With proper guidance and setting, these experiences can be safe and profoundly transformative. Our role as healers is to provide that safe space and guidance, ensuring that participants are supported throughout their journey.

Isabella Rodriguez: How do you ensure the safety of participants during these intense experiences?

Nayeli: Ensuring the safety and well-being of participants during a ceremony is our utmost priority. To start, we conduct a thorough assessment of each individual's mental and physical health. It's crucial to understand their background, any pre-existing conditions, and their intentions for participating in the ceremony. This helps us gauge their readiness and identify any potential risks.

During the ceremony, our role extends beyond just administering the mushrooms. We closely observe each participant, staying attuned to their physical and emotional state. The environment is controlled and safe, designed to provide a sense of security and tranquility. This might include a comfortable physical setting, a calm atmosphere, and the presence of trusted individuals who can offer support.

In moments where a participant might feel overwhelmed or disoriented, grounding techniques are employed. This can include gentle verbal reassurance, guiding them through breathing exercises, or sometimes just a comforting presence. The idea is to help them navigate any challenging aspects of their journey while ensuring they feel supported and safe.

Isabella Rodriguez: Finally, what do you think the wider world can learn from your practices with psilocybin?

Nayeli: Our practices with psilocybin, deeply rooted in tradition and respect for nature, offer valuable lessons for the wider world. One key lesson is the importance of healing in harmony with nature. These mushrooms are a gift from the earth, and they teach us about the interconnectedness of all living things. They remind us that we are not separate from the natural world but a part of it.

Another lesson is the power of introspection and confronting our inner selves. In a world where external distractions are constant, psilocybin ceremonies offer a space for deep self-reflection. They encourage individuals to face their fears, insecurities, and traumas, leading to profound personal growth and healing.

Lastly, there's a lesson in humility and respect for ancient wisdom. Modern society often prioritizes scientific understanding over traditional knowledge. However, these ancient practices have much to offer in terms of understanding the human psyche and our place in the universe. By respecting and learning from these traditions, we can find new ways to address mental health, spiritual emptiness, and the disconnection many feel in today's world.

Isabella Rodriguez: Nayeli, thank you for sharing your wisdom and insights with us today. It's been enlightening to learn about your practices and the profound role of psilocybin in traditional healing.

Nayeli: It's been my pleasure to share. Our traditions are a deep well of knowledge and understanding, and I am honored to pass on what has been entrusted to me. I believe that by sharing our practices, we open doors to greater understanding and respect across cultures.

Isabella Rodriguez: Before we conclude, do you have any final thoughts or messages you would like to share with our audience, especially those who might be considering psilocybin for their personal journey?

Nayeli: I would like to emphasize the importance of approaching psilocybin with respect and an open heart. It's not a shortcut to enlightenment or a quick fix for life's problems. Instead, it's a sacred tool that, when used correctly, can offer profound insights and healing.

For those considering this path, I advise seeking experienced guidance, entering the experience with clear intentions, and being prepared to face whatever may arise. It's a journey of self-discovery that can be transformative, but it requires respect, patience, and a willingness to learn from the teachings it offers.

Isabella Rodriguez: Your insights have been truly valuable, Nayeli. Thank you once again for this enlightening conversation and for sharing the rich traditions of your culture with us.

Nayeli: You're welcome. I hope our conversation today serves as a bridge between worlds, fostering understanding and respect for the ancient wisdom that has much to offer to modern society. Thank you for this opportunity to share.

Outro

Our enlightening discussion with Nayeli provided a valuable glimpse into the enduring traditional practices surrounding psilocybin mushrooms. Her perspective casts these fungi as more than inanimate substances; they are revered as sentient beings imbued with sacred spirits. This respect permeates every step of the ritual, from the moment of gentle harvest to the cups of mushroom tea ceremonially consumed.

Dr. Isabella Rodriguez

The intricacy of preparation reflects the seriousness accorded to these psilocybin journeys. Whether through fasting, prayer, or intention-setting, great care is taken to orient the mind appropriately before embarking on a visionary voyage.

During the ceremony, Nayeli guides participants through difficult moments with compassion. Her goal is not merely pleasant trips but true healing that can emerge from wrestling with one's inner demons. Catharsis, counseling, and collective sharing afterward help integrate these intense encounters into everyday life.

Nayeli's wisdom is a testament to the potential of traditional healing practices in addressing modern psychological and spiritual needs. Her clarification of the misconceptions surrounding psilocybin mushrooms is particularly poignant, emphasizing their role as sacred medicine rather than recreational substances.

Such time-honored practices offer lessons for modern therapeutic contexts. They remind us that healing with psilocybin cannot be reduced to simple drug administration. It requires reverence for the sacrament, trust in the guide, and integration to imbue the experience with meaning.

By illuminating her worldview, Nayeli bridges cultural divides, inviting us to reconsider assumptions about psilocybin's utility and deepen our engagement with traditional wisdom. Her perspective is a humbling yet hopeful reminder that diverse cultures have long cherished and protected access to psilocybin's visionary domain. With care, openness and respect for ancestral knowledge, modern societies may also find healing and renewal through psilocybin's unique consciousness-expanding lens.

CHAPTER 12: Conclusion

The tale of the psilocybin mushroom is one that traverses history, culture, science, and the landscape of the human psyche. This enigmatic fungus has captivated humanity for centuries, playing the role of spiritual guide, therapeutic aid, counterculture symbol, and scientific marvel. Its story echoes our eternal search for meaning, healing, and an expanded understanding of consciousness itself.

Across continents and millennia, indigenous cultures gravitated toward the wisdom of the mushroom. In ritual and ceremony, it opened portals to realms beyond the mundane. The Aztecs venerated it as teonanácatl – flesh of the gods. Mazatec healers relied on its visionary insight for divination and curing. Siberian shamans revered its ability to connect them to the spirit world. Though the rituals differed, there appeared to be a universal recognition of the mushroom's power to catalyze insight and transcendence.

Modernity brought renewed encounters with this ancient sacrament. Scientists like Albert Hofmann isolated psilocybin from its fungal home, creating new inroads into its mysteries through chemistry and pharmacology. Researchers, including Timothy Leary, explored its effects on individual and collective consciousness, for better or worse. And visionary mycologists like Gordon Wasson, Paul Stamets, and Terence McKenna honored the mushroom's legacy while working to usher it into a new era.

Along the way, the story took many twists – hype and scandal in the 1960s, suppression and stigma through the War on Drugs, and the slow recovery of research in the 1990s leading to today's psychedelic renaissance. Yet the mushroom, in some sense, survived these ups and downs, waiting patiently underground for its relationship with humanity to evolve toward wisdom.

Now, as the world awakens to its power once more, the lessons of the past resonate. By integrating respect for traditional practices, open yet critical scientific inquiry, compassion for those who struggle with mental illness, and care in guiding individuals through the psychedelic passage, society can harness the healing currents that flow through psilocybin's kingdom.

There will always be more to explore, understand, and debate about this humble fungus and its outsized influence on the human mind and spirit. Yet one thing remains clear – the psilocybin journey has immense potential for revealing new depths of consciousness, perception, and meaning if we have the courage and care to embark upon it together.

Dr. Isabella Rodriguez

This book is just one small part of an ancient and ever-unfolding story. May it serve as an invitation to those who feel the call to explore consciousness and healing through nature's psychedelic gifts. Soon, new generations of psychonauts, scientists, therapists, and seekers will shape the next chapter of psilocybin's narrative. It is sure to be replete with mystery, promise and timeless lessons about the links between fungi, human culture and the realms of the mind.

APPENDIX: Glossary of Key Terms

5-HT2A Receptor: A subtype of serotonin receptor found in the brain that plays a key role in the effects of psychedelics, including psilocybin.

Alkaloids: A class of naturally occurring organic compounds that contain nitrogen atoms. Psilocybin is one such compound.

Anxiolytic: Referring to the property of a drug to alleviate anxiety. Some psychedelics have shown anxiolytic effects in clinical studies, making them potential treatments for anxiety disorders.

Ayahuasca: A traditional South American psychoactive brew made from plants that contain DMT and MAOIs. It is used for spiritual and healing purposes.

Blind Study: A type of research design where participants do not know whether they are receiving the experimental treatment or a placebo. This is essential in psychedelic research to reduce bias and placebo effects.

Breakthrough Experience: A term often used in the context of DMT or high-dose psychedelic experiences to describe moments of profound insight, transcendence, or the feeling of encountering an ultimate reality or truth.

Cognitive Flexibility: The mental ability to switch between thinking about two different concepts or thinking about multiple concepts simultaneously. Psychedelics are hypothesized to enhance cognitive flexibility, which could have therapeutic implications.

Consciousness Expansion: A term used to describe the sensation of an individual's consciousness extending beyond their normal waking perception, often reported during psychedelic experiences.

Cross-Tolerance: A phenomenon where tolerance to one drug results in tolerance to another drug, typically because both drugs act on the same receptors. For instance, cross-tolerance can occur between LSD and psilocybin, both of which primarily act on serotonin receptors.

Default Mode Network (DMN): A network in the brain that is active when the brain is at wakeful rest and not focusing on the outside world. Psychedelics are known to reduce the activity of the DMN, which is thought to be associated with the experience of ego dissolution.

Dissociative: A class of hallucinogens that can induce dissociation, a feeling of detachment from the self and the environment. Examples include ketamine and PCP.

Double-Blind Study: A study design where neither the participants nor the researchers know who is receiving the experimental treatment and who is receiving a placebo, minimizing bias.

Ego Dissolution: A state often reported during psychedelic experiences where the sense of self becomes diminished or disappears entirely.

Entheogen: A substance, often of plant origin, that is ingested to produce a non-ordinary state of consciousness for religious or spiritual purposes. Psilocybin mushrooms are considered entheogens.

Entactogen: A class of psychoactive drugs that produce experiences of emotional communion, oneness, relatedness and emotional openness—that is, empathy or sympathy—as particularly evidenced by MDMA.

Entoptic Phenomena: Visual effects that originate within the visual processing system of the observer. Psychedelics can amplify these phenomena, resulting in geometric patterns or fractals.

Hallucinogen Persisting Perception Disorder (HPPD): A condition characterized by the re-experiencing of visual disturbances that are reminiscent of those produced by the ingestion of hallucinogenic substances, persisting long after the substances have left the body.

Heffter Research Institute: An organization dedicated to conducting research on psychedelics, primarily focusing on psilocybin, to contribute to the understanding of their potential therapeutic benefits.

Holotropic Breathwork: A practice developed by psychiatrists Stanislav and Christina Grof aiming to achieve altered states of consciousness similar to those of psychedelic experiences through accelerated and deepened breathing.

Hyperconnectivity: A state of increased communication between different regions of the brain, often associated with psychedelic experiences.

Liminal Space: A psychological or metaphysical space where the boundaries between the conscious and unconscious mind are blurred. Psychedelic experiences are often described as liminal.

MAO (Monoamine Oxidase): An enzyme that breaks down monoamine neurotransmitters such as serotonin and dopamine. MAOIs inhibit this enzyme, increasing the levels of these neurotransmitters.

Mycelium: The vegetative part of a fungus, consisting of a network of fine white filaments (hyphae). It is the part from which mushrooms grow.

Neurogenesis: The process by which new neurons are formed in the brain. Some research suggests psychedelics may promote neurogenesis.

Neuroplasticity: The brain's ability to reorganize itself by forming new neural connections. This is believed to be a mechanism through which psychedelics exert their long-term effects.

Neurotransmitter: A chemical substance released at the end of a nerve fiber by the arrival of a nerve impulse and, by diffusing across the synapse, causes the transfer of the impulse to another nerve fiber, a muscle fiber, or some other structure.

Open-Label Trial: A type of clinical trial in which both the researchers and participants know which treatment is being administered. This approach is sometimes used in psychedelic research when a double-blind study is not feasible.

Pharmacodynamics: The study of the biochemical and physiological effects of drugs and their mechanisms of action. Understanding the pharmacodynamics of psychedelics is crucial for their therapeutic use.

Phenethylamine: A class of compounds that includes several psychoactive drugs, including mescaline. They are structurally similar to the neurotransmitter dopamine.

Placebo Effect: A phenomenon where an individual experiences a perceived improvement in condition due to their expectations, not because the treatment itself has any therapeutic effect.

Psychedelic: Referring to a substance that affects the mind, mood, or other mental processes. Psychedelics are a subclass of psychoactive substances.

Psychedelic Afterglow: The residual positive effects that are often felt in the days or weeks following a psychedelic experience, which can include enhanced mood, increased mindfulness, and a sense of well-being.

Psychedelic Integration: The process of making sense of, learning from, and applying the insights gained from a psychedelic experience to one's life. Integration is considered crucial for the therapeutic use of psychedelics.

Psychedelic Renaissance: Refers to the renewed interest and research in the therapeutic potential of psychedelics after decades of stigma and legal restrictions.

Psychedelic-Assisted Psychotherapy: A treatment approach that combines the use of psychedelics with psychotherapy sessions to facilitate healing and personal growth.

Psycholytic Therapy: A form of therapy involving the use of low to moderate doses of psychedelics to enhance the process of psychoanalysis or psychotherapy.

Receptor Agonist: A substance that binds to and activates a receptor, mimicking the effect of a naturally occurring neurotransmitter. Many psychedelics, including psilocybin and LSD, are serotonin receptor agonists.

Serotonergic: Referring to drugs or other agents that produce their effects primarily by interacting with serotonin receptors in the brain.

Recommended Resources

Books:

"Psilocybin Mushrooms of the World" by Paul Stamets

A comprehensive guide to psilocybin mushrooms, including identification, habitats, and traditional uses.

"The Psychedelic Explorer's Guide: Safe, Therapeutic, and Sacred Journeys" by James Fadiman

Offers insights into how psychedelics can be used safely and responsibly for personal and spiritual development.

"How to Change Your Mind" by Michael Pollan

Explores the history and resurgence of psychedelic drugs, including psilocybin, in scientific and therapeutic contexts.

Websites:

Erowid (erowid.org)

A member-supported organization providing access to reliable information about psychoactive plants and chemicals.

MAPS (Multidisciplinary Association for Psychedelic Studies) (maps.org)

Focused on creating medical, legal, and cultural contexts for people to benefit from the careful uses of psychedelics.

Shroomery (shroomery.org)

Provides information about psychedelic mushrooms and offers a community forum for discussions.

Scientific Articles and Journals:

"Journal of Psychopharmacology"

Features studies on the effects of psilocybin and other substances on the brain and behavior.

"Neuropsychopharmacology"

Publishes research on the neuroscience and effects of psychoactive substances.

"Psychedelic Science Review"

Offers reviews of current research in the field of psychedelic science.

Tools:

"Headspace" (Mobile App)

Provides guided meditations that can complement therapeutic work with psychedelics.

"ChemSpider" (chemspider.com)

A free chemical structure database providing access to structures, properties, and associated information.

"PubMed" (pubmed.ncbi.nlm.nih.gov)

A search engine accessing primarily the MEDLINE database of references and abstracts on life sciences and biomedical topics.

ABOUT THE AUTHOR: Dr. Isabella Rodriguez

Dr. Isabella Rodriguez is a distinguished figure in the realm of psychopharmacology, with a focus on the enigmatic world of psychedelics. She earned her doctorate from a prestigious institution on the East Coast, where her groundbreaking thesis explored the neurophysiological impacts of psychoactive substances. Her passion for the field was sparked by a transformative encounter with traditional medicine during her travels in South America, which reshaped her academic trajectory.

Before her foray into the world of psychedelics, Dr. Rodriguez gained recognition for her groundbreaking research in neuroplasticity and its implications for mental health.

Dr. Rodriguez's passion for her field is rooted in a deep-seated belief in the healing power of psychedelics, guided by rigorous scientific inquiry and a respect for the substances' historical and cultural significance. As an advocate for responsible and informed use, she has been a vocal proponent of the decriminalization and scientific exploration of psychedelic substances.

She has contributed significantly to our understanding of the relationship between psychedelics and neuroplasticity, advocating for their potential in mental health treatment.

An advocate for the responsible exploration of psychedelic substances, Dr. Rodriguez has worked with various NGOs and think tanks dedicated to policy reform and scientific research in the field. Her expertise has led her to consult on several interdisciplinary projects, the details of which remain confidential due to the sensitive nature of her work.

Currently, Dr. Rodriguez continues to contribute to the field through her research and as an advisor to emerging scientists and practitioners. Her commitment to advancing our understanding of psychedelics is matched only by her dedication to preserving the anonymity and integrity of her work.

Printed in Great Britain
by Amazon